AN INTRODUCTION TO
PASSIVE HOUSE
BY JUSTIN BERE

Published by RIBA Publishing, 15 Bonhill Street, London EC2P 2EA

ISBN 978 1 85946 493 9

Stock code 79862

British Library Cataloguing in Publications Data
A catalogue record for this book is available from the British Library.

Designed by Atelier Works
Printed and bound by Butler, Tanner & Dennis Ltd, Frome, UK

RIBA Publishing is part of RIBA Enterprises Ltd.
www.ribaenterprises.com

Cover images
Main image:
Bruno Klomfar Photography

Back page – top to bottom:
Edward Hueber/ Archphoto
Bruno Klomfar Photography
Christine Blaser, Bildaufbau-Fotografie
Hanspeter Schiess Fotografie
Langenkamp.dk Architects
Erica Overmeer/Future Documentation

AN INTRODUCTION TO PASSIVE HOUSE

BY JUSTIN BERE

RIBA Publishing

Contents

Foreword

Making convincing solutions visible

I met Justin Bere in November 2008 on a London-bound train during my return from a seminar in Cambridge. An intense exchange of views ensued and continued throughout the journey. The Architect and the Physicist – this mix worked well despite the divergent languages of our very different disciplines. A major problem of modern times is the increasing focus on specialisation with its resulting fragmentation of disciplines and lack of general overview. An architect of the traditional school and a physicist with an established sense of purpose immediately find similarities beyond any technical jargon.

Architecture has traditionally been understood as the task of integrating the different requirements of the built environment into a single object. Architects are thus seen as masters of interdisciplinarity: knowledgeable and competent designers and organisers of the building process. Architects are trusted with the fulfilment of the fundamental objectives of any construction task: ensuring the good health and comfort of occupants, protecting the environment and, last but not least, preserving social peace. Today there exist highly specialised experts for each of these spheres, but according to this traditional view, architects are the generalists.

Physics, on the other hand, has traditionally endeavoured to provide a basic understanding of the processes around us – whether animate or inanimate or man-made. The environment is complex; only rarely does a single isolated event appreciably affect its form and lead to visible transformation. Mechanical forces, gravity, electromagnetism, light, heat and moisture all affect the life cycle of a building. Scientists are seen as the generalists for these natural phenomena.

Generalist meets generalist – the purveyors of responsible architecture and of responsible scientific research should have few difficulties in terms of communication. And this is exactly how our exchange progressed. We soon agreed that it was necessary to overcome short-sighted and unsustainable piecemeal dictates of trends that call for the optimisation of only a few details in isolation – again the result of specialisation and fragmentation.

Today, motivated teams are (again?) able to design, detail and construct buildings in an integrated and holistic manner. With integrated software, the instruments are now available. Buildings can serve their primary purpose while being comfortable, sustainable and energy efficient – and they needn't be expensive either. At the same time, such buildings can exhibit the highest architectural standards. This book is full of such examples. No one should try to tell us that the above are contradictory objectives; these objectives only become contradictory when dealt with in isolation by experts wearing blinkers who lack integration expertise.

Passive House relies on the communication and integration capability of enlightened and receptive people. If such teams do not lose sight of their goals and make use of the tools provided by the ever-growing Passive House community, then the construction of buildings in which the energy consumption no longer plays a role will become a "piece of cake". Buildings that consume just a tenth of the energy conventionally consumed can be reliably planned using the Passive House planning tool; such minimal energy consumption ultimately becomes insignificant. This results in buildings that are simpler, more reliable, longer-lasting and more comfortable, in addition to solving the issues of energy supply and environmental impact.

In this book, Justin Bere elaborates on these ideas using the language of an architect accented by numerous photos, drawings, and examples. He rigorously dispels widespread misconceptions and shows how Passive House opens new possibilities for creative design. I hope that this book finds many readers who will walk away inspired and motivated by the examples portrayed in it.

Dr Wolfgang Feist,
Founder and Scientific Director of the Passivhaus Institut, Darmstadt

Wolfgang Feist giving a seminar at the Muse, London, June 2009
Clockwise from left: Henrietta Lynch, Mark Siddall, Matthias Kaufmann,
Wolfgang Feist, Alan Clarke, Darren Oldfield, Andrew Farr, Justin Bere,
Sarah Lewis. Also present: Bill Bordass

Preface

Searching for integrated design in the 21st century

The best Passive House architects are masters of integrated design, searching for aesthetic beauty on the one hand and technical excellence on the other. No longer can it reasonably be considered adequate for buildings to look good in photographs while performing badly in terms of their comfort or resource consumption. I believe clients expect their buildings to perform well, and are becoming much more demanding about this – and so they should be.

The light-filled, graceful, flowing spaces produced by architects such as Alvar Aalto, Louis Kahn, Frank Lloyd Wright and Le Corbusier were, in part, the result of the monumental social progress that occurred during the 20th century. However, if modernism was also dependent on an abundant supply of cheap heating fuels and the invention of the refrigeration cycle to maintain habitable conditions in buildings such as glass skyscrapers with their otherwise uncontrollable solar gains, then we would need to re-consider the merits of such an environmentally calamitous approach to design.

But passive building techniques enable us to create very comfortable, light-filled buildings that operate with the minimum of energy. Passive House is emphatically not a product, nor does it require designers to use particular products. The Passivhaus Institut offers manufacturers technical assistance to improve their products, and provides quality assurance certification, but Passive House buildings can be built without any certified products.

Passive House is a standard and an advanced method of designing buildings using the precision of building physics to ensure comfortable conditions and to deeply reduce energy costs. It removes all guesswork from the design process. It does what national building regulations have tried to do. Passive House methods don't affect "buildability", yet they close the gap between design and performance and deliver a much higher standard of comfort and efficiency than government regulations, with all their good intentions, have managed to achieve.

When we use Passive House methods, we learn how to use insulation and freely available daylight, in the most sensible way and in the right amounts for both comfort and energy efficiency. This is, I believe, fundamental to good design, and is the next step we have to make in the evolution of our dwellings and places of work. The improvements that are within our grasp are potentially transformative for mankind and the planet. In its driving vision, it could be argued that Passive House picks up threads of the late 19th-century Arts and Crafts movement including its associations with economic and social reform, rejection of energy-consuming and polluting industrial processes, and its reappraisal of the value of people-centred design and skilled local labour.

Passive House buildings make it possible, and economically viable, to use entirely locally produced renewable energy to operate buildings throughout the year. Reducing energy demand is a key component of the energy revolution that is occurring in Germany and Austria, where both countries appear to be on target to run their economies on 100% renewable energy by 2050. Renewable energy can meet the summer energy needs of buildings in most climates, but for renewable energy to meet winter demand a truly low energy approach is needed. Without closing the "winter gap" between demand and supply, the energy revolution can only be a dream. As Wolfgang Feist explained in his plenary speech at the 2013 International Passive House Conference in Frankfurt, in an ordinary low-energy house in Northern Europe, even a massive 95m² of solar PV panels would result in a large "winter gap" in which demand for heat energy significantly outstrips the supply capability of the PV panels. Such a large gap cannot economically be met by inter-seasonal storage in the foreseeable future. By contrast, renewable energy from 41m² of solar PV panels is already enough to make a Passive House almost completely energy-independent in Northern Europe, even in the winter months. The tiny heat demand of a Passive House reduces the "winter gap" to such an extent that seasonal storage is economically feasible to make up any shortfall. So Passive House and on-site or local renewable energy systems are perfectly matched to support the 21st-century energy revolution.

"Positive feedback loops drive growth, explosion, erosion, and collapse in systems" – so wrote Donella Meadows in 1997. "A system with an unchecked positive loop ultimately will destroy itself. That's why there are so few of them." Meadows advocated writing clever rules for self-organisation in order to avoid runaway systems, and this is exactly what the Passivhaus Institut has done with the Passive House Planning Package (PHPP). Clever rules help us to build low-energy buildings, without compromising our enjoyment of comfortable dwellings, so helping us to reduce the depletion of the natural capital of the planet.

Passive House and the energy revolution give us, for the first time, the opportunity to hold on to the social progress that has been made and to the uplifting aesthetic tenets of the very best 20th-century buildings, while at the same time transforming our technical abilities to make social progress and beauty possible in a world where excessive consumption is no longer tenable.

So we can make enjoyable, long-lasting, comfortable and efficient new buildings, and we can improve old buildings so that they too are comfortable, healthy, and operate with minimal energy consumption and minimal carbon emissions. This might seem like a daunting task; indeed, many architects still seem to think that the perfect integration of art and science is too difficult, too costly or even impossible.

However, this book is intended to blow apart that belief and to highlight just a few of the most attractive Passive House designs from around the world. Each building has been chosen to act as a beautiful signpost to an exciting future, showing the emergence of a new approach in which Passive House design can help our species coexist with all the other precious species in a spectacular natural world that is so utterly dependent upon each and every one of us, and upon which we are more dependent than many people recognise.

As Passive House methods become better understood, architects are emerging who can integrate inspirational design and energy efficiency. A great 21st-century building provides real shelter without relying on the excessive, expensive and carbon-emitting energy consumption of old-fashioned, fossil-fuel-thirsty heating and cooling equipment. A great 21st-century building is one that is beautiful to look at but that also feels good in reality when the power supplies are turned down to almost nothing. The printed page cannot adequately describe what it feels like to be in a building. In a Passive House all the senses are pampered while using only tiny amounts of fossil fuel. People report feeling "just right … never too cold and never too hot … never too dry and never too humid", and "the air always feels fresh … you come back home and the bedroom feels aired; you never get that musty smell that you get in an ordinary house."

I fear that some architects give more priority to how their buildings will look in architectural magazines than to making sure that their buildings perform efficiently and comfortably for the benefit of their occupants. Like an iceberg, much of what is important about a building is out of sight – and we ignore that fact at our peril.

But architects and services engineers increasingly label their buildings "passive", "passive solar", "zero carbon", "carbon positive", "plus energy" or even "active". This is good because it suggests the emergence of a growing interest in building performance. However, I would question, based on the performance results that are consistently reported by post-occupancy investigators and building physicists, whether the tools used by many designers are up to the job of giving them a reliable means to design integrated, efficient buildings. Indeed, some methodologies seem to me to be no more substantial than slogans. I would say to the sloganeers, "here's the Passive House data, where's yours?" The reason Passive House methods are creating such a stir is, I believe, that people see they get something substantial in return for using Passive House methods: an assurance that their designers will produce quality buildings that are comfortable and can use virtually no energy; designs that accurately predict future performance and comfort in the hands of the average building user.

The results we are getting from Passive House buildings in the UK are indeed so good that they are unprecedented in the context of our construction industry, and reports indicate that this also applies to the uptake of Passive House in most other climates around the world.

But remember, architecture must also provide visual enjoyment to be successful, and this is why I hope that the Passive House projects in this book will offer some encouragement to talented young architects interested in making the integration of design and ecology mainstream in the 21st century.

Replacing guesswork with calculation

In their book The Autonomous House (1975), Brenda and Robert Vale indicated that conservatories or "winter gardens" were in their opinion one of the most appropriate energy-saving technologies to use in the UK climate, but they pointed out that occupants had to use winter gardens intelligently otherwise they would fail to produce the desired energy savings – and could, in the wrong hands, lose more energy than they gain. The risk was that occupants would use the winter garden as a space to live in and heat on overcast days in the winter months, and in the end it would be a net emitter of energy in the heating season rather than a net harvester of energy. Nevertheless, the solar winter garden concept was often considered to be a fundamental component of pioneering energy-saving buildings throughout the 1970s, 80s and 90s.

However, in the same book Brenda and Robert Vale also described one project, St George's School in Wallasey, Cheshire, designed in 1960 by architect Emslie Morgan, which "has, in fact, no more than a very large double glazed window across the south side of the building … the building is well-sealed to reduce the number of air changes per hour to one or less." The Vales went on to say that "the internal temperature of the building could be maintained without any external power sources apart from electricity in the lights, and although a backup system was originally installed by the local authority it was later removed after it was found to be unnecessary in the extremely cold winter of 1962–3." However, the building's ventilation rates were too low to maintain fresh air in a school, and the Architects' Journal in 1969 doubted the validity of the method.

When starting to think about designs for my own experimental low-energy house in the period 2000 to 2002, neither Max Fordham or I knew anything of Wolfgang Feist's new Passive House concept. Yet when I asked Max Fordham how I could achieve the great results of the Wallasey School, but without the problem of stale air, Max told me without hesitation that I obviously needed to put some kind of heat-recovery ventilation system into the house. In an email to me in August 2002, he told me that "the most important thing is for the building to be airtight". He went on to advise: "meet the Building Regulations ventilation requirements with a warm-air heating system, which provides fresh air via mechanical ventilation with heat reclaim. Control of this is critical. The fan should run on boost for dealing with cooking smells. Then generally at half speed to save electricity unless the heating demand cuts in." Max's ideas, which I adopted in the Muse, were remarkably similar to Wolfgang Feist's concepts carefully set out ten years earlier. I mention this story because it shows just how logical such an approach was to Max Fordham even without knowing about Wolfgang Feist's work. However, unable to afford the cost of a services engineer to produce my calculations, I used guesswork for the detailed design. The Passive House software, however, now provides an affordable way of replacing guesswork with calculation.

The Muse, Newington Green, London; design without PHPP calculations

What is Passive House?

Introduction

Passive House (also referred to as Passivhaus) is a standard and a scientific design tool that achieves exceptionally comfortable and healthy living and working conditions combined with low energy demand and minimal carbon emissions. It can be used for all building types, including very low-cost buildings. The techniques work for both new and refurbished buildings of all types and sizes. The Passive House method has been successfully applied and tested across all European climates, the US, Canada and even in warm Asian climates where there is a cooling requirement. Indeed with some regional variations of the design techniques, the method has been shown to be applicable almost all around the world. The design techniques originated in the central European climate with its very cold winters, but local weather data is always used to tune passive buildings into their precise location, and performance monitoring has shown that Passive House is ideally suited to the milder climate of the British Isles.

A Passive House building is one in which thermal comfort (as described in international standard ISO 7730) can be provided by post-heating or post-cooling of the fresh-air flow that is required for good indoor air quality, as defined by DIN1946. This is achieved without recirculating used air which even now remains common practice in most air-conditioned office buildings (W. Feist: Passive Houses in Practice. Bauphysik Kalendar, Ernst & Sohn, Berlin 2007).

This definition doesn't contain any arbitrary numerical values, and is valid for all climates. It is a fundamental concept and not a randomly set standard. The concept requires the use of precise technical methods, which are based upon the science of building physics.

Passive House delivers much of its comfort and very low energy costs by means of insulation and draught-free construction. If a building isn't ventilated by draughts, then it must be ventilated by another means and a passive house uses heat-recovery ventilation to provide ample fresh air in winter, when the windows are closed, without wasting energy from cold draughts blowing through the building. An ordinary building also extracts stale air directly to outside, wasting all the heat contained in the air. In a passive house, the extracted air gives up most of its warmth to the fresh air supply. The supply of healthy quantities of fresh air without wasting energy is sometimes described as "hygiene ventilation". Winter warmth is also partly provided by passive use of solar energy and partly by making use of internal heat sources such as people and appliances. After all this, the resultant annual heat demand is tiny by comparison with an ordinary building.

Passive House methods provide an accurate way of designing buildings. Using the Passive House Planning Package (PHPP), developed by the Passivhaus Institut (PHI) in Germany, a good designer and builder can create comfortable, healthy, economical, environmentally friendly and affordable buildings.

The methods were first tested and proven in the Europe-wide CEPHEUS research programme. Outstanding results have also been found within the current Building Performance Evaluation programme funded by the UK's Technology Strategy Board. Test results show that Passive House buildings create the perfect conditions for living comfortably, healthily and cheaply, with minimal energy demands, whatever the weather is doing outside.

New window inventions, heat-recovery ventilation products and other manufactured products have been stimulated by the uptake of Passive House methods across Europe. Alongside the uptake of Passive House methods, it is only a matter of time before suitable high-quality products from local manufacturers appear; supporting and regenerating the local economy. More can be learnt by referring to Passipedia, at: www.passipedia.org

The origins of Passive House – how and why it began

After the forests of Europe had been mostly destroyed for agriculture and firewood, Europeans turned to coal for fuel as the Industrial Revolution started. But where coal wasn't available, other ideas emerged. For example Icelandic people turned to burning peat in their turf-walled and turf-roofed houses. For stability the walls were very thick, and these turf walls were found to have good insulating qualities so that hardly any heating fuel was required. These Icelandic homes were a simple form of early passive house. There are many other similar stories of the discovery of passive building techniques around the world, especially in some of the world's gentler climates, but the real challenge that began to be addressed by researchers from the 1960s onwards was how to replicate this passive performance in European and North American buildings where people had steadily rising comfort requirements and consequently very high winter heating demands.

In Sweden during the 1960s, a civil engineer named Bo Adamson carried out research on highly insulated buildings and built a first prototype development to test his ideas at Alhem. By the time of the oil crisis in 1973, and partly due to Adamson's work, Swedish buildings were relatively energy efficient compared to buildings in most of Europe, and by the mid-1980s low-energy design had become a legal requirement (SBN80 Swedish Building Regulation 1980) for new buildings in Sweden and Denmark. Also at this time, Adamson was teaching holistic design methods to architecture students at the Faculty of Engineering at the University of Lund in Sweden, where he was at the same time working on further developments in insulation, thermal bridging, insulated glazing, airtightness and controlled ventilation. Adamson's ambition was to find a way of building that required no heating at all. To achieve this aim he assumed that it would be necessary to allow temperatures to drop to perhaps 17°C in a Swedish winter.

Project of 32 houses in Alhem, by Bo Adamson for Skellefteå Power

This was the approach Adamson took on a theoretical project in China in 1986–7 when he collaborated with the Chinese Ministry of Construction on a feasibility study of passive houses in southern China. It was illegal to heat buildings south of the Yangtze river at that time, so his proposal had no heating but high levels of insulation, high build quality and triple glazing. New houses at the time had indoor temperatures as low as freezing point during the winter, and Adamson was asked by the Chinese government to carry out research on passive houses with the aim of suggesting ways to improve the indoor winter temperatures of unheated Chinese buildings. The results of his research, a publication on passive and low-energy houses in southern China, can be found in the BKL construction library, Report TABK—92/3006, 1992.

Dr Wolfgang Feist – "the father of Passive House"

Meanwhile during the 1980s Wolfgang Feist, a young German physicist with a master's degree in Quantum Mechanics and later a Doctorate in Architecture, was carrying out low-energy building research with the aim of finding a method to create very low-energy passive buildings which did not compromise on the warm indoor temperatures and general comfort that people in Europe had become used to. Feist felt that maintaining people's comfort was essential if people were to be convinced by the proposal to save energy, and in this respect his approach differed from the approach taken in China. Feist quantified the energy losses in a building, to minimise those losses and to quantify the resulting energy requirements to maintain 20°C, after using all the free heat gains available.

Feist visited Sweden frequently throughout the 1980s to share his ideas with Adamson. This appears to have been an exciting time in which the two men systematically and urgently laid the foundations of the Passive House concept. Feist's work involved computer simulation of the heat balance of a building, hour by hour during a typical year. He was looking for a robust methodology to apply to all forms of building, guaranteeing the highest level of comfort while using only negligible amounts of energy.

It was clear from the beginning that the Passive House concept had to be cost-effective. This is why Feist and Adamson concentrated on the building envelope. Walls and windows are fundamental components of buildings, so improving them is a cost-effective starting point. Moreover, if improvements to the fabric are made by means of industrial manufacturing processes, the resulting efficiencies act against price increases. An example of this is that the cost of triple glazing in mainland Europe is now only €12 per square metre more than double glazing after starting off costing €80 more.

In May 1988, while working at Lund with Bo Adamson, Dr Feist launched the definition of "the Passive House". Passive Houses were defined as: "buildings which have an extremely small heating energy demand even in the Central European climate and therefore need no active heating. Such houses can be kept warm "passively" by using the existing internal heat sources and the solar energy entering through the windows as well as by the minimal heating of incoming fresh air."

By 1989 Dr Feist completed his work in thermal building simulation at the University of Kassel and immediately formed a small consortium to fund and build the first test-project; a Passive House apartment block at Darmstadt Kranichstein.

Over 20 years of monitoring of the four completed dwellings has shown that the pilot project has consistently achieved 90% annual energy savings compared to the German Building Code of 1995, while maintaining excellent comfort and exceedingly healthy living conditions.

After the outstanding success of the pilot project, Dr Feist founded the Passivhaus Institut in 1996, in Darmstadt, Germany to research energy use in buildings, to develop design tools such as the Passive House Planning Package (PHPP) and also to be the scientific head of the CEPHEUS EU-wide building trials (1997).

Wolfgang Feist emerged as the father of the Passive House movement because he developed the scientific foundations of the standard and then went on to form the Passivhaus Institut. Feist, more than anyone, tirelessly works both scientifically and politically to explain the clear social and economic benefits of the standard in a way that can be understood by everyone. He has always been realistic about the challenges, political and financial, that will be faced by such a socially liberating movement. A solution that reduces energy consumption, even though providing clear benefits to people and the environment, will not be championed by those who profit from poor-quality construction or by those who see energy efficiency as a threat to business-as-usual. Nevertheless Dr Feist is successfully leading a worldwide revolution that has the potential to put power and security back into the hands of local communities.

The pilot Passive House building

In 1989, Dr Feist brought together a team of three private individuals and an executive architect in order to test the practical feasibility of the Passive House concept by means of a pilot Passive House building at Darmstadt Kranichstein, Germany. A scientific research group was formed and the research included developing:

- an efficient heat-recovery ventilation unit
- new specially insulated window frames and blinds
- construction details for the connection of building components
- solar heating technologies and a concept for heat recovery from waste water

The house was given extremely good insulation and efficient heat-recovery ventilation, and achieved a pressurised n_{50} air test result of less than $0.3h^{-1}$. The energy-monitoring results proved that the strategies were very successful. The measured net energy consumption (space heating + domestic hot water + electricity), averaged across the four houses, showed that the buildings required almost no heating at all (below $10W/m^2$). This represented a saving of 90% compared to the German Building Code of 1995. The pilot houses also required much less energy for domestic hot water and electricity than an ordinary dwelling due to solar water heating and very efficient electrical systems and appliances. Dr Feist and his family are so happy with the great success of the project that they still live in one of the four houses.

The theoretical proof for the feasibility of such houses was provided in Wolfgang Feist's thesis Passive Houses in Central Europe (1993), in which he analysed the characteristics of each building component by means of computerised simulations. For example, in his thesis Feist demonstrated how the then new technology of low-emissivity coatings in triple glazing enabled large glazing areas to reduce the annual heating needs of a European house, assuming a very draught-free construction.

The pilot Passive House building, Darmstadt Kranichstein, 1991

Testing the concept at scale – the CEPHEUS project

Building upon the success of the pilot scheme, in 1997 a second, larger project of 22 very low-cost Passive Houses was built at Wiesbaden. In fact, they were the lowest-cost houses built in the town at the time. Subsequently, 32 low-cost passive houses were built at Hanover Kronsberg under the programme known as Cost Efficient Passive Houses as European Standards (CEPHEUS).

On the left, Wiesbaden low-cost Passive House homes, 1997
On the right, Hanover Kronsberg low-cost Passive House homes, 1998

Five countries (Germany, France, Switzerland, Austria and Sweden) were involved in this first large-scale performance test of cost-efficient passive houses. Fourteen different projects, comprising a total of 250 passive house dwelling units, were built in the CEPHEUS programme.

In-use energy monitoring was carried out in 114 of the CEPHEUS dwelling units. The average specific heat demand was found to be 16.6kWh/m²/yr. Some households naturally used more energy than this, and some used less. The resulting ogee or S-shaped curve of the graphed data is not exclusive to passive houses. The same shape of graph, but with a much wider distribution of results, was found to apply to ordinary German Building Code houses. Comparing both sets of results revealed that the average annual heat-energy consumption of a passive house home was about one-tenth that of the average use of an equivalent ordinary German Code home, or one-fifth of the average use of an equivalent "low-energy" German Code home.

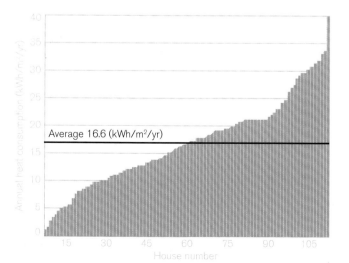

The CEPHEUS programme – average heat energy use was as predicted

The impact of building users on design energy targets

When the CEPHEUS results for passive house buildings were plotted on the same graph as older buildings and those classified by the German Building Codes as "low-energy buildings", it was found that even the highest consumer of heat energy in a passive house building used less energy than the lowest consumer in a "low-energy building" as defined by the German Building Code.

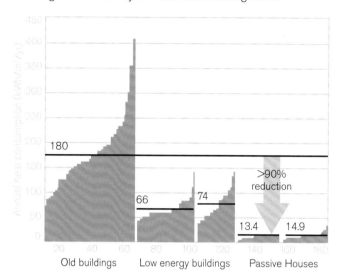

The CEPHEUS programme found that even the highest consumer of heat energy in a Passive House building always used less energy than even the lowest consumer in a "low-energy building"

The CEPHEUS energy-performance results illustrated the benefit of the Passive House method in robustly bringing down the running costs of a building, almost regardless of occupant behaviour patterns. While it is clear that building users do have an impact on energy use in a Passive House just as in any other type of house, the CEPHEUS findings showed that the "Performance Gap" is closed because the impact of a user upon the designed energy use of a Passive House is much less than the impact of a user upon the designed energy use of an ordinary building (Ref: CEPHEUS Final Report. Passive House Institute/ Stadtwerke Hannover, 2001; Scientific guidance and evaluation, PHI 2001).

The economic foundations of Passive House

The Passivhaus Institut (PHI) in Germany has based the economic foundations of the Passive House standard on "capitalised costs" alternatively referred to as "lifetime costs". Here is an introduction to the theory. (Also, refer to page 29 for futher information on the "whole-life cost" of Passive Houses in the UK.)

It could be argued that the problem of low-energy buildings is that a reduction of energy consumption is achieved only at the additional cost of enhanced building quality (eg extra insulation, more panes of glass in better-quality frames, greater care to achieve better airtightness, better-quality materials and more energy-efficient ventilation systems).

However, the capital cost of a building is only part of the lifetime cost of a building, and if energy costs to run the building over its lifetime are considered there are lifetime cost advantages in spending some extra money on the construction of the building. The question is what is the optimum formula for the lowest lifetime cost?

When the theory of the economic foundations of Passive House was formulated in 2001 it was calculated that the energy-saving benefits of an ordinary low-energy house, based on 2001 energy prices, was found in a building that consumed around 40–50kWh/m²/yr specific space-heat demand. Reducing energy demand further was not justified from the point of view of economics alone, because it simply increased the whole-life cost of the home.

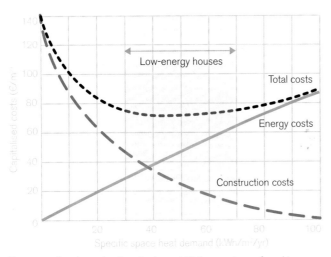

For conventional construction, the lowest lifetime costs are found in a building that requires 40–50kWh/m²/yr heat energy

However, a Passive House was found to change this conclusion because, since the peak winter heat-energy demand in a Passive House is so low, a Passive House does not need a conventional heating installation. It was calculated that, using local weather data, it is possible to deliver sufficient heat to maintain steady indoor winter temperatures of 20°C in the coldest days of winter by means of the heat-recovery ventilation system.

The capital cost savings that result from this approach bring down capitalised or whole-life costs, with the result that the lowest whole-life cost was found in a Passive House building that consumed just 15kWh/m²/yr specific space-heat demand.

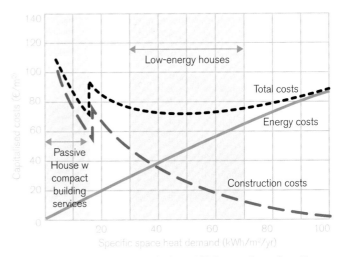

For Passive House construction, the lowest lifetime costs are found in a building that requires just 15kWh/m²/yr heat energy

Since 2001, when interest rates were still at 5% and energy costs in Europe only 4 cent/kWh, the situation has become even more favourable for the passive house approach. With more up-to-date figures of 3% interest rates and energy costs of 9 cent/kWh, the "conventional optimum" will be 17 or 18kWh/m²/yr specific space-heat demand (roughly the same as a Passive House), without even without taking into account the Passive House cost advantage of simpler systems.

The Passive House solution

The following pages explain the key elements that are normally needed to achieve the Passive House standard.

To be clear, though, Passive House is not a product, nor do certified Passive House buildings need to contain certified products.

Passive House is primarily a technical design method, based on the fundamentals of building physics, and represented by the Passive House Planning Package (PHPP), which is tuned by the architect to the average weather conditions of each building's location.

Passive House architects are free to develop their own design strategies, as long as they comply with the requirements of building physics, to create warm, comfortable, dry buildings that are also economical to run. The PHPP enables architects to achieve these requirements with as much certainty as physics can provide.

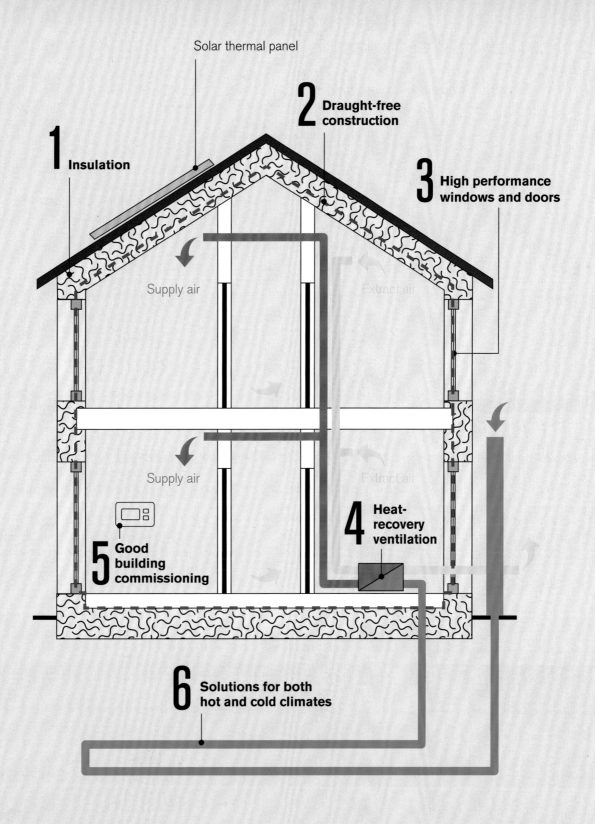

Solar thermal panel

1 **Insulation**

2 **Draught-free construction**

3 **High performance windows and doors**

Supply air

Extract air

Supply air

Extract air

5 **Good building commissioning**

4 **Heat-recovery ventilation**

6 **Solutions for both hot and cold climates**

Key elements of the Passive House standard

The key purpose of a Passive House is to achieve a very high level of indoor comfort and health, whilst using very little heating or cooling (maximum 15kWh/m²/yr "specific heat demand") and very little total energy, taking into account transmission losses from a power station (maximum 120kWh/m²/yr "primary energy demand").

The Passive House Planning Package (PHPP) contains detailed requirements that must be fulfilled in order to achieve the mandatory comfort, health and energy standards for certification. To achieve all the detailed technical requirements of the PHPP software, the following methods form the essential basics of Passive House design.

1 Insulation

External insulation is typically around 200–400mm thick in Passive Houses in temperate climates. It helps minimise cold bridging and protects the building fabric from thermal stress and from weathering. It can be made from wood or mineral fibres, or from foam boards. It is suitable over masonry or timber construction, and can be finished in a variety of ways, including render or wood.

For a thinner wall or roof, insulation is commonly integrated within timber-framed construction. In this case a breathable insulation made from wood or mineral fibre, combined with vapour-breathable airtightness and weather membranes is a good solution. Well-designed and constructed timber walls need no chemical treatment and are a robust and healthy solution for occupants and the environment.

In retrofit work, internal insulation is often used in order to avoid changing the external appearance of a building. Vapour-permeable wood-fibre insulation at a maximum thickness of around 100mm is widely regarded as a good solution that buffers peak moisture loads in a room while maintaining sufficient vapour drive to avoid condensation within the fabric. This solution does not normally provide enough insulation for a Passive House in a temperate climate, but may be enough for the Passive House Enerphit standard. In 2013 a new vapour-permeable foam insulation product was launched, containing capillary-active straws to maintain vapour-permeable walls and protect against damp and mould growth.

Cold bridging is calculated with proprietary software such as Therm, Heat2, Heat3, Bisco or Trisco, and the results of each external condition or junction in the building are required to be entered into the PHPP software.

As well as fabric insulation, pipework and some ductwork must be very well insulated and mounting brackets should minimise cold bridging. Cold surfaces must be wrapped with insulation that is impermeable to vapour (to avoid condensation on the pipes) but hot pipework can be wrapped in vapour-permeable insulation.

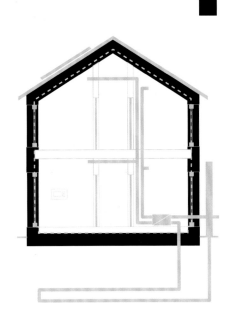

Timber frame is a space-efficient option

Wood-fibre insulation is suitable for interior or exterior use

Draught-free construction

Draughts, both from leaky fabric, and from crude bathroom extractor fans, can waste a large proportion of the heat generated to warm a building. Avoiding cold draughts saves energy and improves occupant comfort. If users feel even slight draughts, or cold feet, this may have a range of consequences, from raised heating set-points to switching on local electric heaters. So even subtle draughts from leaky building fabric or primitive "trickle ventilation" gaps in window frames, (both permitted by the UK Building Regulations) may contribute to create a large gap between a building's design expectations and its actual performance.

Draught-free construction is not as difficult as it is often made out to be. It simply requires care from the design team and care from the construction team. Draught-free construction is as much the responsibility of the architect as it is the responsibility of the contractor.

It is essential for the "line of airtightness" to be considered from an early design stage in order to ensure that the designer makes it reasonably possible for the contractor to carry out a first air test at an early stage of the construction process, and in order to avoid unecessary complications and delays to the construction process. It is essential that the first air test is carried out as soon as the windows and doors are installed and before internal finishes cover over the designated line of airtightness. The reason for this is the simple trick that if the line of airtightness is visible at the first air test, any defects can be found and repaired.

Once a first-stage air test is successfully achieved, any degradation of the air test, usually caused by faulty mechanical or electrical service penetrations, can be monitored and rectified by a second stage or final air test.

With appropriate care and the application of advanced installation techniques, it is easy to achieve airtightness at least 17 times better than the UK Building Regulations normally require. More information on the techniques can be found in Airtightness Report, practical guidance to achieve excellent levels of airtightness in Passivhaus building fabric (available free on the Research page of the bere:architects website).

Once this level of fabric integrity is achieved, it is necessary to be equally careful and methodical in the application of heat-recovery ventilation to maintain hygienic air quality in the winter months when windows normally remain closed.

Using airtightness tapes to fit a window

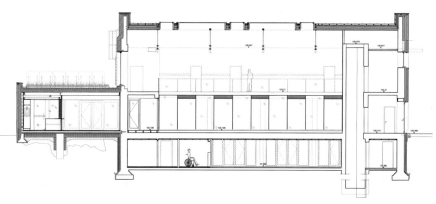

Line of airtightness shown in a general arrangement drawing

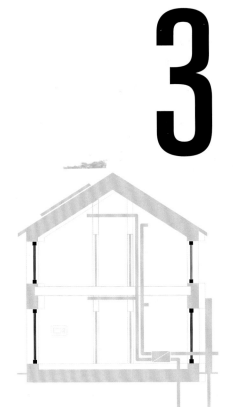

3 High-performance windows and doors

The primary reason for very high-quality windows and doors is to provide thermal comfort and eliminate the risk of condensation and mould growth. Triple-glazed Passive House windows are different from ordinary triple-glazed windows in several respects.

Passive House window frames have insulating properties that make them almost as warm as the high-performance glazed component of the window.

Passive House windows are almost totally draught-free. The glass fits into the frames without any air leakage and the frames utilise continuous seals (without joints), usually in two "lines of defence"; they are precision-engineered to fine tolerances and use easily adjustable hinges for fine-tuning of the installation. They use multi-point locking systems in order to ensure that the window is pulled firmly against the seals in the closed position without distortion. This also helps provide superb security.

A Passive House window is designed to maximise solar gains to help warm a building in winter. This is achieved in spite of the three layers of glass, by using unusually clear glass, defined by its "G-value", which is the amount of solar heat energy that enters through a window as a proportion of the total energy that reaches the window. A higher G-value represents a higher transmission of solar heat into the building. Even the light of an overcast winter day can provide useful gains in a building that hardly needs any heat energy at all.

A Passive House window must be installed correctly. Each certified window design has installation advice to achieve its designed thermal performance. Some window designs rely on being installed in "pockets" which reduce heat loss and make the frames look thinner and more elegant. Windows must be fitted using advanced techniques such as special screws that do not distort the outer frame, and the junction between the window and its opening in a wall or facade system must be absolutely airtight. Twin barriers (usually high-performance tapes) are usually used on the inner and outer faces of frames to control air and moisture movement.

Summer shading may be necessary if the design includes a large amount of glass facing towards the midday or afternoon sun. The PHPP software for the project will highlight if this is an issue of concern. Where it is, it is best achieved with retractable external venetian blinds, but appropriate internal blinds can also reflect about 40% of the sun's heat, and sliding or folding external screens can also be used for architectural effect.

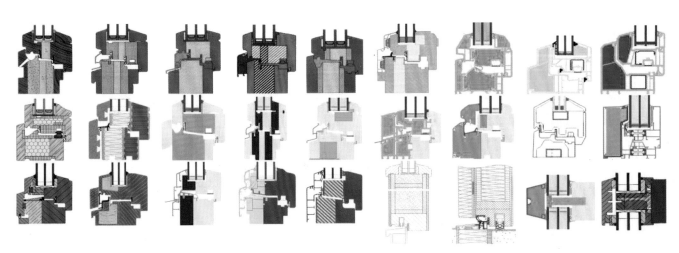

The Passive House requirement for insulated, airtight window frames has already resulted in a huge outburst of creative energy

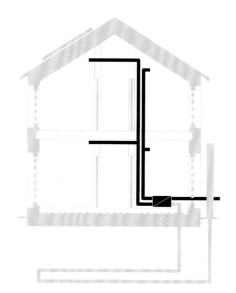

Heat-recovery ventilation

Heat-recovery ventilation, sometimes described as "hygiene ventilation", provides plentiful fresh air for both domestic and non-domestic Passive House buildings. This is especially useful in winter so the well-sealed windows don't need to be opened, completely avoiding cold draughts, condensation and mould growth. Well-designed, installed and commissioned heat-recovery ventilation saves around 90% of the heat in the stale air extracted from bathrooms and kitchens. The recovered heat is put into the fresh incoming air that is supplied to living spaces and bedrooms. It is an energy-saving requirement and is also essential for good winter air quality in a draught-free building (also see page 40).

Once you are used to the concept, it seems incredible that ordinary houses use basic bathroom extractors that throw out precious heated air without saving the heat, and suck icy draughts into the house, while a boiler burns large quantities of fossil fuel to try to put things right! Most ordinary non-domestic buildings are also almost as primitive in their approach to ventilation.

Heat-recovery ventilation equipment consists of tiny, electrically driven, energy-saving fans to gently feed ventilation air through filters and a passive heat exchanger at just the right speed for both indoor air quality and efficient heat recovery. They use only about 35W of power in a domestic application, and over the course of a year can save ten times as much energy as they use. In a house they run 24 hours a day, but in a non-domestic building it is important that they are commissioned to run only during hours of occupancy, otherwise the Passive House primary-energy limit is likely to be exceeded. They are not dependent on wind velocity or thermosyphonic drive as some non Passive House systems are. They operate silently and reliably, removing stale air and filtering out dust.

There is new evidence that heat-recovery ventilation systems improve indoor air quality in urban locations. Airborne particulates are thought to be a cause of heart attacks, strokes and asthma, and in a study carried out by the Institute of Environment and Health at Cranfield University (2013), the Passive House domestic dwelling at 4 Ranulf Road was compared with a conventional house 100 metres along the road, and the Passive House was found to have half the level of fine PM2.5 particulates compared to the conventional house (more information on the Research pages of the bere:architects website).

Both domestic and non-domestic Passive House buildings always supply 100% fresh, filtered, outdoor air to the interior spaces via their heat-recovery ventilation systems. These systems are very different from the recirculation systems used in ordinary commercial buildings throughout the world, which provide an inferior form of heat recovery by means of returning warm, used air back into the building.

While in winter up to 90% of the waste heat is saved by means of a passive heat exchanger, in summer an automatic bypass is often used, and users can feel free to open the windows as they would in an ordinary building.

It is possible that manufacturers will continue to find cost advantages in developing ventilation units that combine with hot-water production and backup heating, and that this will also simplify controls strategies and commissioning and maintenance regimes in the future. In effect these units could become single-point operating units, no more complex or expensive than a washing machine if they are produced in sufficient quantities.

A non-domestic heat-recovery ventilation unit

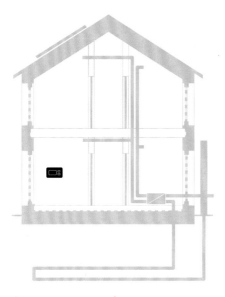

5 Good building commissioning

An essential part of the design team's role is to check that the mechanical and electrical systems of a building have been installed properly and are working in the way that they were designed. It is also important to check energy and water consumption and ventilation flow rates once the building is in use. Passive House designers are usually passionate about keeping control systems and user interfaces as simple as possible. Building Management Systems (BMS) are generally considered a completely unnecessary complication. Current research across the full range of non-domestic buildings funded under the UK Technology Strategy Board's Building Performance Evaluation Programme is revealing that BMS systems are the cause of irreconcilable problems in almost every building being monitored. Of the buildings being monitored, only the Passive House Mayville Community Centre is free of a BMS system and only the Mayville appears to be living up to the performance promised in its design. Passive House is largely about keeping things simple and about quality control!

Careful checking of a building's commissioning can be a satisfying conclusion to a project

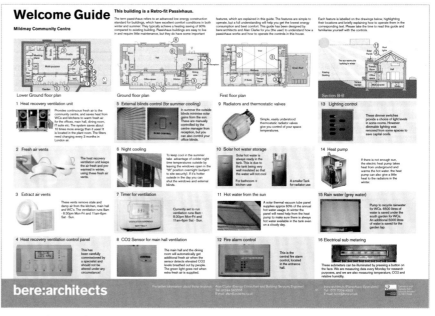

Example of a User Guide to help occupants understand their building

6

Solutions for both hot and cold climates

Passive House techniques are already common in Germany, Austria, Switzerland and Belgium, and well tested throughout Europe including the UK and Ireland. The climate has important differing local characteristics even across central and northern Europe, so it is essential that the correct local climate data is used. But Passive House techniques are applicable globally, and local climate data might for example result in some regions requiring even better windows or other regions requiring less good windows. However, the Passive House principle remains the same – only the details need to be adapted. With appropriate details, Passive House buildings can be used to reduce heating-energy demand in cool climates or to reduce cooling-energy demand in warm climates. In both cases, the governing principle is that the demand is so small that the gentle ventilation system can be used to deliver the necessary energy to provide thermal comfort.

In warm climates, Passive House methods are now successfully being used to reduce the peak cooling load of buildings. Appropriate size and quality of windows, shading and the reduction of internal heat loads by using highly energy-efficient equipment all serve to minimise the amount of cooling energy that might still be needed to supply good indoor air quality.

Increasingly, the Passivhaus Institut is working on prototype projects that are compatible with local building traditions and climatic conditions. Some remarkable projects in warm climates were presented at the 2012 International Passive House Conference in a session dedicated to "passive houses in warm and hot climates". Papers were presented on the performance of a terraced Passive House in Spain; a new Austrian Embassy in Jakarta, Indonesia; and a Passive House for hot and humid southern China. Friends and former staff have projects under way or planned in hot climates around the world – in Turkey, Oman, Korea and Ghana.

Jürgen Schneiders of the Passivhaus Institut in 2009 produced a useful study called Passive Houses in South West Europe. This was followed in 2012 by a collaborative research publication from the Passivhaus Institut titled Passive Houses for Different Climate Zones. The results of these research projects are also included in the new PHPP 8 release.

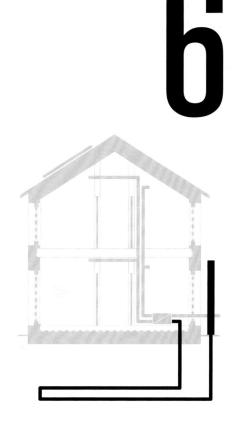

A new Passive House in Spain

Passive House Austrian Embassy in hot and humid Jakarta, Indonesia

Why Passive House?

The renewable-energy revolution

I would like to start by looking at how Passive House can help to deliver a renewable-energy revolution.

Passive House makes it possible to reduce energy demand by up to 90% compared to ordinary buildings. Reducing energy use, mainly in the building and transport sectors, is a key component of the energy revolution that is happening in Germany and Austria – both countries appear to be on target to run their economies on 100% renewable energy by 2050. Renewable energy can meet the summer energy needs of buildings in most climates but without closing the "winter gap" between demand and supply, the energy revolution can only be a dream. As Wolfgang Feist explained in his plenary speech at the 2013 International Passive House Conference in Frankfurt, renewable energy from 41m^2 of solar PV panels is enough to supply a Passive House with renewable energy throughout the year in a temperate climate. So Passive House and on-site or local renewable energy systems are perfectly matched to support the 21st-century energy revolution.

Energy independence is potentially a huge benefit to a nation's security and to its economy – and the evidence from Germany and Austria is that this can probably can be achieved without the environmental damage of extracting and burning fossil fuel.

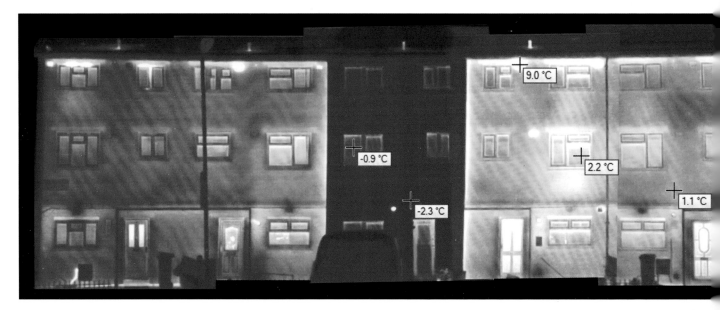

Comfort and health

Because Passive House buildings are so cheap to run, they offer affordable comfort. They provide warm and dry spaces in winter, without any condensation at all, and are always full of fresh air. Recent research compared the level of PM10 and PM2.5 particulates in the air of a Passive House and in the air of a neighbouring conventional house (see page 36). It was found that the air inside a Passive House is likely to provide significant health benefits for its users, especially helpful for asthma sufferers and those who have heart or lung conditions.

Harriet McKerrow of Arup used a Building Use Studies (BUS) occupant satisfaction survey to analyse the new Passive House at Ranulf Road in Camden (see page 39), and the house was found to perform well above the usual benchmarks in many respects including overall user satisfaction. Evidence of people's enjoyment of living in Passive House buildings, and evidence of the health benefits that they are experiencing, can also be seen in a number of interviews of residents in passive house buildings on the Films page of the bere:architects website.

As late as December 2012, the Mayville Centre Passive House retrofit in London required no heating whatsoever, yet indoor temperatures were still around 22°C. At the same time monitoring was undertaken of two small, un-improved solid-wall apartments adjacent to the centre and it was found that, even with some heating (which the residents said they could barely afford) the un-insulated flats both had dreadful condensation problems and were struggling to maintain temperatures of 16 or 17°C.

By contrast, people who visit Passive House buildings always seem to be struck by how simple and normal, and how quiet and calm they seem – and how warm they feel in the winter months. Occupants often say how they never feel too warm or too cold, and say how they appreciate the quality of the air in Passive House buildings.

Affordability

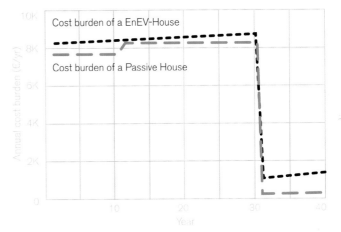

The German government offers a Passive House low interest loan

Assuming that the additional cost of building a Passive House home compared with an ordinary home is around 8%, let's also assume that the additional investment is financed through a higher mortgage loan, resulting in slightly higher repayment costs. It is estimated that for a house of approximately 150m², and an interest rate of 4.7% and 1.6% repayment rate, there might be an additional annual repayment rate of €945 euros. However, in Germany the house builder or owner can apply for the Development Loan Corporation's "Energy-efficient construction ESH50/Passivhaus low-interest loan", which reduces the annual cost burden in the first few years to almost compensate for the additional investment. Additionally, due to the lower annual energy costs of a Passive House compared to an ordinary building, the annual cost burden of a Passive House is lower than that of a normal house. After 30 years, when the cost of the mortgage has been completely repaid, the family will profit from the extremely low energy consumption. Moreover the occupants no longer have to worry about increasing energy prices and such low energy demand can be supplied with renewable energy (Ref: Active for more comfort – The Passive House. PHI/International Passive House Association).

Most UK buildings are draughty, have only single glazing and very little insulation. The Marmot report of 2011, The Health Impacts of Cold Homes and Fuel Poverty, is a vivid portrayal of the health impacts of living in cold, damp homes. The Passfield Drive Retrofit for the Future project used thermal imaging to illustrate the improved comfort and likely health benefits derived from using a range of Passive House methods on an old building including external insulation, triple-glazed windows, heat-recovery ventilation and the elimination of cold draughts (bere:architects, 2011)

Those in the developed world who question the "affordability" of Passive House should consider the whole-life cost benefits of reduced energy demand. The available options come down to choices between short-termism (buying an energy-inefficient house and then having large energy bills each month) and long-termism (spending more per square metre on the house, but saving money through low bills). As the German government loan system shows, policy can help individuals take a long-term view.

Short-termism has caused us to extract and burn the earth's coal and oil reserves with massively damaging environmental consequences over a period of just a few generations. With hindsight, that was unaffordable.

A sustainable, long-term approach

In Pathways to 2050: Three Possible UK Energy Strategies, a report published in February 2013 by the thinktank British Pugwash of the Pugwash Conferences on Science and World Affairs, it is stated that during the next 40 years the UK will have to rebuild its energy-supply infrastructure and it is calculated that if low-energy retrofit can be reduced to £20,000 per dwelling by scaling-up our ambitions, this is less than one sixth of the cost of building a low-carbon electricity supply by 2050.

The Passive House approach can be applied to such a programme and would enable us to maintain or achieve high levels of comfort affordably while reducing our consumption of irreplaceable resources.

It seems obvious which path we should follow in an objective, ethical world. Even if we aren't convinced by ethics or moral principles, we should be worried by the risk of the "perfect storm" of challenges that we are frequently warned about, should we continue with "business as usual". As Richard Branson says on the cover of his latest book, "Screw business as usual." If we are warned about the risks ahead but choose to ignore them, then we participate in a huge gamble for the opportunities available to future generations. Building Passive Houses or refurbishing buildings to the Passive House standard will not solve all these problems at once, but they are very positive first steps in trying to avoid them.

Embodied energy

The Passive House methodology requires the use of the Passive House Planning Package to accurately measure energy flows in a building. PHPP is primarily an energy modelling tool. It does not measure embodied energy or whole-life costs, but it does not preclude these important aspects of design either.

The Passive House methodology is complementary and compatable with low embodied energy. Pages 30–33 are devoted to the synergy between Passive House and concepts of local construction and low embodied energy.

Saving money – whole-life costs

When considering the cost of purchasing any product, it surely makes sense to take into account the lasting financial impact of its operation and maintenance.

In spite of this, the main deterrent for constructing low-energy buildings is the associated increase in build costs (Schnieders and Hermelink, 2006; Kansal and Kadambari, 2010; McManus et al., 2010). However, increased upfront costs in a low-energy building are likely to be offset by reduced energy bills during the building's life. This can be defined numerically using the concept of Whole Life Costs.

Whole Life Costs (WLC) is defined as follows:

WLC = Purchase Cost + Energy Bills + Non-Energy Bills + Maintenance Costs

In the first UK study to try to quantify these savings using the concept of "Net Present Value" (Passivhaus buildings: Case study evidence for reduced whole life costs, Caroline Johnstone and Nick Newman, bere:architects, 2011, available on the bere:architects Research pages) the authors applied a wide variety of scenarios of gas prices, electricity prices and interest rates to the whole-life costs of a real Passive House building. The conclusions indicated that Passive House buildings were financially viable in all of the scenarios except for when there were continued very high interest rates, and they clearly show that strong benefits are derived even if one excludes the presumed increase of energy prices. So current research is showing that Passive House is the most cost-efficient standard unless energy prices are half of what they are in 2013 (Ref: W. Feist in: International Passive House Conference 2013, Proceedings, PHI 2013. Research Group on Cost Efficient Passive Houses 42, PHI, Darmstadt 2013). Interest rates are unlikely to alter this since the consensus is that they will not rise dramatically for the foreseeable future.

Overcoming the performance gap

The fact that UK buildings have such a poor record of achieving their performance targets is well documented by research from British universities and other research organisations such as the Building Services Research and Information Association (BSRIA) and the Usable Buildings Trust. Further information can be found on the www.usablebuildings.co.uk events resource page. Research carried out by the Carbon Trust's Low Carbon Buildings Programme 2006, and latterly research being carried out by the Technology Strategy Board, regularly finds energy consumption two to three times higher than design intentions, and in the worst cases actual energy consumption is missing design targets by a factor of five. There are many reasons for this, some of which are out of the control of designers. For example, design-and-build contracts in the UK may enable contractors to change the architect's design and substitute poorer-quality products.

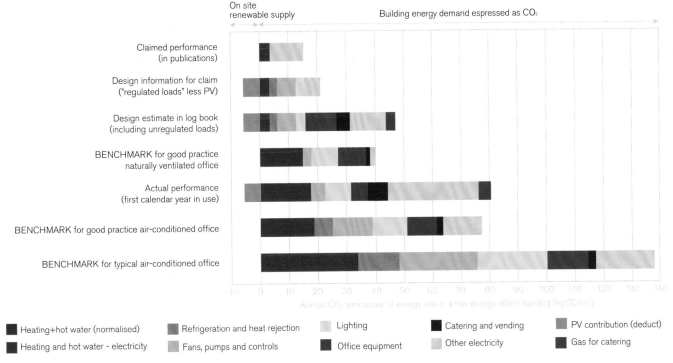

On site renewable supply

Building energy demand espressed as CO_2

- Claimed performance (in publications)
- Design information for claim ("regulated loads" less PV)
- Design estimate in log book (including unregulated loads)
- BENCHMARK for good practice naturally ventilated office
- Actual performance (first calendar year in use)
- BENCHMARK for good practice air-conditioned office
- BENCHMARK for typical air-conditioned office

Annual CO_2 emissions of energy use in a low-energy office building (kgCO/m²)

- Heating+hot water (normalised)
- Heating and hot water - electricity
- Refrigeration and heat rejection
- Fans, pumps and controls
- Lighting
- Office equipment
- Catering and vending
- Other electricity
- PV contribution (deduct)
- Gas for catering

However, procurement methods apart, the graphs on page 15 show that designers can take action to reduce the performance gap. While some of the variance from design will always be due to "unregulated loads" that were not predictable, much of it is not. According to Roderic Bunn (BSRIA), research has consistently found that building designers have not calculated very well because the tools they were using to predict energy consumption were not very suitable for the job. In light of these results, I think it is reasonable to suggest that if your design methodology does not work for the average user, don't blame the user, instead change your design method.

Accurate calculation is exactly what the Passive House Planning Package facilitates, and evidence of this has been found in practice both in new and retrofitted UK Passive House buildings as a result of research projects carried out with UK Technology Strategy Board funding. Early results indicate that the use of Passive House methods has a strong tendency to create buildings that are performing as well as, or even better than, the design model predicted – and the Passive House design targets were much more ambitious than the current UK Building Regulations, and even exceed the UK government's 2016 "zero-carbon" standard.

The publication of such results leaves little ambiguity over how to narrow the gap between design and performance. Passive House can reduce a new or refurbished building's energy consumption in the hands of an average user by between 50% and 90% in actual use.

Carbon-emission reductions

In proportion to their energy efficiency, Passive House buildings achieve significant in-use carbon-emission reductions compared to the carbon emissions of ordinary buildings. The difference widens when it is understood that ordinary buildings commonly strongly underperform against their design ambitions, whereas Passive House buildings tend to perform close to design ambitions.

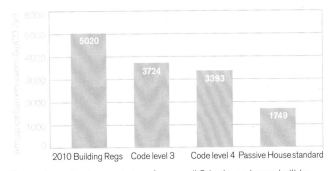

Comparison of carbon emissions for a small 3-bedroom house built to four different environmental standards, based on Larch House Ebbw Vale (source bere:architects)

Designed for United Welsh Housing Association as a prototype for social housing, the Larch House at Ebbw Vale, Wales (2010) demonstrated how Passive House can achieve "zero carbon" status according to Code Level 6 of the UK Code for Sustainable Homes, using only on-site renewables

Political incentives – lessons from Austria

Like Germany, Vorarlberg has the serious 21st-century goal of becoming self-sufficient in energy by 2050. In the past few decades, this region of Austria has managed to reinvent itself, bringing concepts of sustainability, efficiency and self-sufficiency to the forefront of public consciousness. Strong political signals have given people the confidence to invest in new, sustainable business enterprises and redevelop older ones. Very high regional prosperity, strong sustainable manufacturing output and low levels of unemployment are all indicators of success in the region, and Vorarlberg has become one of the wealthiest areas in the world with an average regional productivity per inhabitant of €31,000.

So what does this mean at the scale of an individual construction project in Vorarlberg? To illustrate this, let me introduce the drivers behind the Ludesch Community Centre, a case-study featured project.

In response to a request from the local authority, the Ludesch Community Centre project by Hermann Kaufmann was included in the Building for Tomorrow programme, which was established in 1999 as part of a research and development programme titled Technologies for Sustainable Development, funded by the Austrian government. Based upon the Passive House concept, the programme is aimed at promoting energy efficiency and the use of renewable energy sources, as well as the adoption of renewable and "green" building materials. Furthermore, it seeks to develop methods for comparing usage patterns and price structures between energy-efficient and conventional construction methods.

The selection of building materials at the Ludesch centre supported regional economic activity; the use of native timber; the protection of exterior timber surfaces by roof overhangs rather than the use of wood coatings; the use of insulation made from renewable resources; and the avoidance of PVC, solvents and other harmful substances.

Such visionary, politically led incentive programmes are intended to address the perceived environmental imperatives whilst also encouraging investment in research and education. As well as being good for the environment, the foresight of Vorarlberg politicians and public has also succeeded in creating a massive growth in 21st-century, sustainable jobs in skilled manufacturing and in sustainable-energy consulting. There is now a strong market for exporting the products of their "green" industry, and this has brought inward investment for their green products and inventions.

Vorarlberg is now home to numerous manufacturing companies producing goods that are consciously aimed at making the region entirely self-sufficient in everything that it needs, from food to homes. Even manufacturing will be run on 100% renewable energy by 2050, and will

source locally grown raw materials wherever possible. At the same time, Vorarlberg is providing excellent education and healthcare for everyone, high salaries and reasonable working hours and a high quality of life in a caring, sharing community. Many of the prosperous Vorarlberg companies remain compact and family owned, but most seem to be competing on the world stage as well as supplying their services locally. The result of such holistic political planning is that relatively little needs to be imported to this increasingly wealthy region.

Many other countries, including the UK, seem to be on a less promising trajectory. Even so, there remains an opportunity for change to reduce the UK's demand for energy to a sustainable level for a green energy-supply system, and I believe that the German and Austrian energy transition plans could be replicated in the UK and a green economy could deliver a transformation of the UK's economic prospects.

Why aren't all buildings built like this?

The main benefits are:
- High levels of comfort, no cold draughts, no cold feet.
- Healthy indoor conditions with no mildew
- Plenty of fresh air and less indoor air pollution
- Reduced environmental impact
- Local economic benefits
- Freedom from energy imports

Passive House is sometimes perceived by those who haven't used the technology as being too restrictive, but the aesthetics of a Passive House are not prescribed by the Passive House software. An inefficient shape or other factor can be compensated for by additional measures – and this can be established at the earliest stages of design, enabling a capital-cost and operational-cost assessment to be made of the implications of any advantageous or disadvantageous design decisions. Used wisely, the Passive House software provides a fundamentally careful and caring approach to building that underpins an architect's personal approach to design.

What the Passive House software does not do, however, is tick off a list of tenets or a set of necessary "ingredients". There are no fixed design features. Instead there are carefully measured quality-control requirements like the prevention of cold bridging and draughts, the recovery of heat from ventilation and the intelligent use of the free energy of the sun. There is little or no restriction to designing beautiful buildings as long as they are designed and built very well – like a machine, or a natural organism. Why aren't all buildings built like this?

Capital and whole-life costs

The whole-life financial costs of "affordable" Passive House new-build dwellings in the UK context has been investigated and compared with the whole-life costs of similar houses that are built only to the current Building Regulations statutory minimum standard. A study produced by bere:architects in 2010 (after the completion of the Welsh social-housing prototypes) attempted to illustrate the expected running costs of a Passive House compared to a minimum standard Building Regulations house. The quantity surveyor Richard Whidborne contributed to the research.

Larch and Lime House social-housing prototypes, Ebbw Vale, Wales, used to model the cost of building affordable Passive House homes

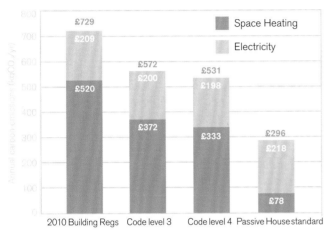

Comparing calculated energy costs of houses built to UK Building Regulations / Code for Sustainable Homes and Passive House

The graph shows what it theoretically costs to fuel a Passive House compared to three other design specifications. While PHPP was the tool used to make these calculations, it should be noted that the in-use difference between an ordinary building and a Passive House may be even larger than the graph shows due to the greater "performance gap" likely between design and actual use of the ordinary buildings (see pages 15, 26, 27).

The social-housing prototypes at Ebbw Vale were used to model a comparison of the cost of building an affordable Passive House home in the UK compared to a standard Building Regulations house type. The research showed that after 19 years the sum of the build cost and running costs of a Building Regulations house will have exceeded that for a Passive House, and that is without factoring in any increase in energy prices.

Subsequently a case study led by by Caroline Johnstone with bere:architects investigated evidence for reduced whole-life costs. Using the definition

Whole Life Costs = Property Purchase Price + Energy Bills + Non-Energy Bills + Maintenance Costs

the research concluded: "The study clearly shows that Passive House buildings are financially viable in all situations except in a scenario where very high bank interest rates negate the substantial energy savings."

In 2012, research was carried out into the capital cost of the Passive House refurbishment of the Mayville Centre It was found that the cost of a basic Passive House refurbishment with a gas boiler was just 3% more than if the building had been built to the minimum Building Regulations standard. Yet this small additional cost had achieved 95% total energy saving over the first winter of operation, whilst at the same time raising indoor winter temperatures to a very comfortable and steady 20–22°C.

Large energy savings achieved at such small extra cost suggest, where fuel has to be imported, that strong national balance-of-payment benefits will accrue in the medium term, and explains why Germany and Austria provide a mixture of financial incentives and statutory requirements to deliver longer-term national benefits.

An example of succesful state inventive is the German Federal State Bank's "Energiepashaushalt 40/Passivhaus credit which provides a 50,000 Euro loan, a 100% disbursement and 2.1% interest rate for each unit built to the Passive House standard".

For further information, refer to: Feist, W. Is it profitable to build a Passive House?, Passive House Institute,2007, http://www.passivhaustagung.de/Passive_House_E/economy_passivehouse.htm

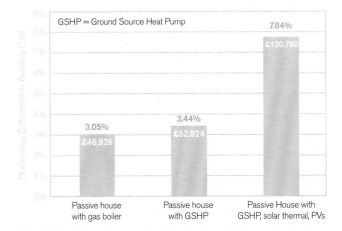

Calculated additional cost of retrofitting the Mayville Community Centre to the Passive House standard compared to UK Building Regulations

Localised Passive House construction
by Thomas Stoney Bryans

Since the Industrial Revolution, construction has been increasingly emancipated from the constraints of the natural world, as we have transitioned from an era of building with labour and materials that were close at hand, to building with whatever we desired from a global marketplace. The inevitable consequence has been a detachment of both architects and society at large from the physical impacts of our buildings on the planet. In specifying steel from China, stone from Italy or tropical hardwoods from South America, we are blind to the impact of their extraction, and to the emissions that result from their production and transportation. If we choose to ignore these environmental costs, we may wish to consider that these processes also have social and economic impacts on the region in which construction is happening. In other words, both jobs and capital – which would once have stayed in the local area – are exported elsewhere.

These challenges may seem distant from the practice of architecture, but they are fundamentally architectural ones – for the potential of the profession to effect change lies in its ability to leverage the act of construction to benefit not just the end user but also the environment and the communities in which construction and extraction occurs. For this to happen, architects need to conceive of buildings not as isolated entities but rather as organisms that are fundamentally integrated into the ecosystems in which they operate. This requires a comprehensive approach to design, one that considers a building's connections to the environmental and human ecosystems around it: the energy and nutrient flows of the environment, and the social and financial capital flows of human creation.

While the Passive House methodology addresses only operational energy and not embedded energy, it nonetheless provides one of the strongest foundations that we have to develop more comprehensively sustainable architectural strategies. By building upon it – firstly by assessing whole-life energy flows, then whole-life nutrient flows (such as construction materials, water cycles and green roofs), and finally by considering a project's impacts on the social and financial capital flows of which it is part – Passive House can act as the core of a more holistic approach to design.

Two houses constructed in Ebbw Vale in Wales – bere:architects' Larch house and Lime house – demonstrate the potential of exactly such an approach. The designs are the culmination of a vision that saw them as a seed for a regional, low-carbon construction industry, utilising local materials and creating local employment. With the specification of Welsh-grown timber, Welsh-made slates, and local stone, for example, the project not only minimises the embodied energy of its construction but also ensures that those materials, as biological nutrients, can remain local when the houses reach the end of their lives.

Such a localised focus is at the core of the international Transition Town movement: a network of communities, from towns to cities, each working to develop resilience in the face of peak oil, climate change and economic instability. As Rob Hopkins, founder of the Transition Network, has written, "The Holy Grail … from a Transition perspective, would be a building that is built to Passive House standards yet uses mostly local building materials". It is an approach that embodies the "Heavy-Near, Light-Far" paradigm of Jason McLennan, where anything heavy – such as building material – is local, whereas things that are "light" – ideas, images, information – can travel great distances. It is a significant shift from today's "Heavy-Far, Light-Far" globalised market and has profound implications for architecture, demanding both local adaptation and design intelligence in materials specification.

While the Passive House standard does not demand any particular construction system, an analysis of both embodied energy and nutrient flows will often favour biological materials such as timber, largely due to inherent carbon sequestration and local availability. Both the quality and quantity of available timber, however, varies enormously from region to region. Within Europe for example, some countries, such as Finland and Sweden, have 75% forestry coverage or more, while the UK by contrast has just under 12%. Such variation in timber availability has a significant impact on the potential of localised supply chains and the products that can be produced. The use of solid-core timber panels for instance has grown considerably across Austria, Germany and Scandinavia since its emergence in the mid-1990s, but due to the enormous volume of material it requires it would clearly be ill suited to wide scale use in a British context.

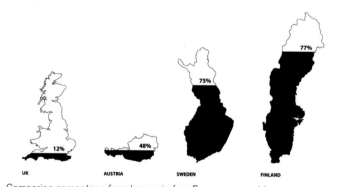

Comparing percentage forest cover in four European countries

For many regions, low-grade timber or restricted supply will demand greater innovation in detailing and construction. The framing system for the Ebbw Vale houses, for instance, was guided by the availability of only small-section low-density Sitka spruce, which had a maximum section size of 215mm. With a requirement for 400mm of insulation, due to the cold and exposed site, a traditional stud frame would have been impossible and the timber-frame manufacturer was not equipped to make the frame from engineered ladder-frame components. A solution was therefore devised with a 215mm stud filled with Welsh Rockwool, with 100mm of wood-fibre insulation on each side.

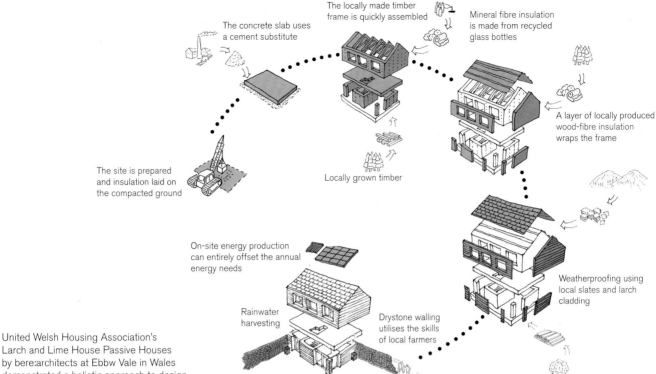

The concrete slab uses a cement substitute

The locally made timber frame is quickly assembled

Mineral fibre insulation is made from recycled glass bottles

A layer of locally produced wood-fibre insulation wraps the frame

The site is prepared and insulation laid on the compacted ground

Locally grown timber

Weatherproofing using local slates and larch cladding

On-site energy production can entirely offset the annual energy needs

Rainwater harvesting

Drystone walling utilises the skills of local farmers

United Welsh Housing Association's Larch and Lime House Passive Houses by bere:architects at Ebbw Vale in Wales demonstrated a holistic approach to design.

A greater challenge for the Ebbw Vale project, however, was that of getting Passive House certified windows locally made, and from local materials. To do so required bringing together a consortium of Welsh timber industry bodies, joinery firms, a window designer and a German window manufacturer, along with the architects, to collectively develop a certified product within two-and-a-half months. Made from thermally modified Welsh larch, the windows of the Vale Passive Window Partnership are today one of the only fully UK-made (as opposed to UK-assembled) Passive House windows available. Such a proactive procurement process may be unusual, but in doing so bere:architects were fully engaged with both the social and financial flows of the human ecosystem of which the project was part, using the act of construction – and the investment that it was bringing – to provide the opportunity for long-term benefits for the wider community.

As a collaboration between a number of different manufacturers, all producing the same product but with locally available materials, the window partnership demonstrates the potential of what Pooran Desai and Sue Riddlestone describe as a "bioregional network":

> Local and regional scale (rather than global scale) technologies can form the basis of a new industrial revolution. There are many opportunities for bulky commodity products, which are expensive to transport, to be produced locally on a decentralised basis. We can set up co-ordinated networks of local producers, responsive to local needs

Desai and Riddlestone's BioRegional charity (best known for its "One Planet Living" framework) has developed a number of commercial enterprises, including paper

mills and charcoal manufacturers, all based on this decentralised model. With a central coordination system enabling them to operate as a single supplier, small producers are able to access large-scale retailers and markets that would otherwise be unattainable. The potential environmental, social and economic benefits that such networks and regional supply chains can produce are profound. They reduce transportation distances and emissions, create more sustainable nutrient flows through the use of locally available materials, create new jobs, develop stronger communities and enable money to stay in local economies for longer.

Through the act of specification, architects, consciously or not, play an active role in the design of supply chains and in the sites of material extraction. As Bernard Planterose, an expert on Scottish forestry, has written, "We specify the timber and we specify the forest together". For local and regional-scale supply chains to be adopted across the construction industry will therefore require a step change in the way that architects design and specify buildings. It demands that all conceivable impacts of a project on the human and environmental ecosystems around it be considered and actively calibrated, rather than left to chance. Such a comprehensive approach to design is not easy, but projects such as the Larch and Lime Houses demonstrate the potential wide-ranging positive impacts that it can bring. For, regardless of how large or small a project may be, every piece of architecture is an organism that is connected by flows of energy, nutrients and social and financial capital to its surrounding ecosystems. If each project is to give back more than it takes from those ecosystems, localised Passive House construction is a good place to start.

The Nirvana of Zero-Zero – energy efficiency and low embodied energy
by Gareth Roberts of Sturgis Carbon Profiling

Buildings by their very nature always consume resources and energy in their construction, and whilst in recent years progress has been made in reducing the operational emissions of buildings, progress on the materials front appears to have been much slower.

The "embodied" carbon emissions that come from the making and maintenance of buildings are significant enough that for many high-performance, low-energy new homes being built today, a greater proportion of their emissions will be put into the atmosphere through their construction than will be consumed over the lifetime of their use.

Experience of assisting architects with reducing the embodied carbon of their projects shows that the task is relatively simple if the designer includes the following five important considerations in the design of a building:

1: Do more for less – Using less material is one of the simplest ways to improve a building's carbon footprint, as this avoids excess waste as well as reducing transport emissions.

2: Select alternative materials – Many materials have similar performance and aesthetic properties but have very different carbon impacts. Designers should select the best material for the job with regard to the lowest carbon impact.

3: Use low-carbon industrial processes – Even the same material can have a very different carbon impact depending on the source of energy used to make it; so, where possible designers should source materials manufactured using renewable energy or from countries with low-carbon grids.

4: Use materials that absorb carbon – Materials such as timber effectively lock away carbon from the atmosphere, which helps a designer to reduce a building's footprint. However, care should be taken to give timber products long-term uses in order to lock the carbon out of the atmosphere for as long as possible.

5: Use locally produced materials – This reduces carbon emissions that arise due to transportation.

In the projects that SCP have worked on over the past four years, it has been possible to reduce the whole-life footprint of most buildings by 30% without adding anything to the construction costs. These savings are achieved by working on the procurement of the materials sympathetically, without affecting the nature of a building's design.

Taking a whole-life view of the emissions associated with a building also helps to clarify other important carbon issues such as: What is the relative impact of transport, waste and site equipment? Is a long-life material better to specify rather than a short-life one that has lower carbon impacts? This approach also puts into perspective the importance of being able to recycle a building's components at the end of its service life.

Architects should give serious consideration to minimising the embodied energy of their buildings' fabric as well as the energy consumption of those buildings, in order to maximise the whole-life benefits of the energy-saving measures deployed in them.

Whole-life design assessment of bere:architects' BRE Watford Passive House Project

SCP collaborated with bere:architects on the 2012 Building Research Establishment (BRE) Passive House competition to build a new house prototype suitable for widespread adoption by both the private and rented social landlord sectors, at the BRE Watford Innovation Park. The competition-winning design shows our latest thinking in reducing the operational and embodied carbon impacts of new housing. The aim was to deliver an affordable and easily maintained, easy-to-operate building to what the team refer to as a "Zero-Zero Whole Life Standard".

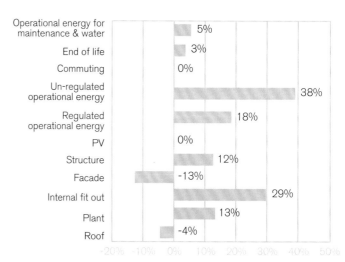

Life-cycle carbon emission of building components

In the table, each main building component is analysed to give an idea of the contribution it makes to the overall carbon footprint of the building.

Elements which are negative are those which have the net effect of taking carbon from the atmosphere rather than emitting carbon into it. Most of these beneficial components are made from timber or from natural insulation, where the absorption of carbon occurs during the growth of the natural material.

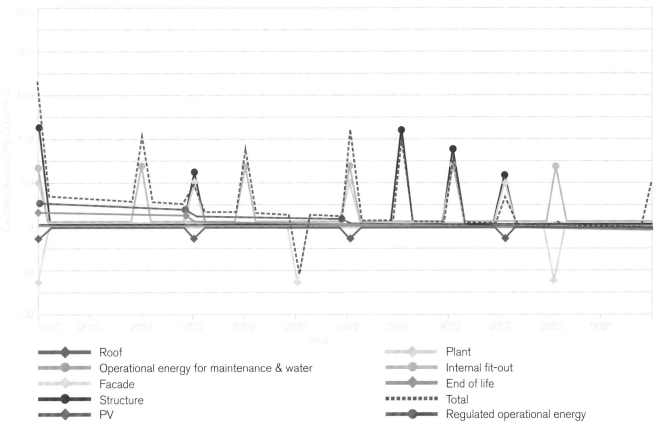

Roof
Operational energy for maintenance & water
Facade
Structure
PV

Plant
Internal fit-out
End of life
Total
Regulated operational energy

Modelling the carbon-emission stream of a building

The graph above shows the modelled emission stream that belongs to the winning design. The model spans a period of 60 years and identifies opportunities for minimising whole-life carbon emissions due to maintenance operations, as well as the interdependencies of different components and the identification and elimination of "weakest links". Weakest links are defined as small components of a design which, if they fail, require the wholesale replacement of other building parts to be undertaken. An example of this might be buried mechanical or electrical services that would require the removal of building plasterboard finishes in order to allow a repair to be carried out.

As the design develops for this project, SCP and bere:architects will develop the specification such that for every one of these houses built in the future, the net result will be to reduce the total amount of carbon being put into the atmosphere to the absolute minimum possible, taking into account both embodied and operational energy seen as a whole.

Whole-life carbon assessment

Although not yet part of the mainstream construction process, whole-life carbon assessment was, in 2012, being considered by the UK government's former chief construction adviser, Paul Morrell. Meanwhile, an EU methodology has arrived in the form of the CEN/TC 350 standard for sustainable construction, which provides a consistent approach to measuring the whole-life carbon emissions of building projects throughout Europe.

The first stage of CEN/TC 350 encompasses the extraction of raw materials, their transportation to a point of manufacture and the process of transforming them into construction products.

The second stage involves the transportation of construction products to site and the on-site processes involved in assembling them into a building.

The third stage covers the maintenance, repair, replacement and refurbishment cycles of a building as well as the use of energy and water during its lifetime.

In the final stage, the building is deconstructed and its redundant components transported off site, processed and either disposed of or reused.

At each of these stages, whole-life carbon analysis can identify solutions with lower carbon impacts than the traditional processes, delivering considerable savings.

Benefits from Zero-Zero thinking

- Delivering the greatest possible carbon savings at the lowest cost
- Highlighting the benefits of selecting natural products that contain carbon taken from the atmosphere
- Providing a quantifiable basis for materials selection
- Highlighting the carbon cost of maintenance and repair

Performance data and user feedback – comfort, health and energy efficiency
by Sarah Lewis

Since the completion of Dr Feist's pilot project in 1991, performance monitoring has been carried out on hundreds of Passive House projects around Europe, and the finding is that Passive House techniques consistently result in buildings that are performing to, and often even better than, design targets. This section looks in detail at some of the techniques used to assess the performance of low-energy buildings. It presents some analysis of the results obtained from three of the first batch of Passive House projects to be built and monitored in the UK: the Ranulf Road Passive House, the Mayville Centre and the Princedale Road social-housing retrofit; all London projects.

The main techniques are grouped into two basic categories: (1) fabric performance and (2) in-use performance (the latter heading includes both energy consumption and user surveys).

Fabric-performance measurements

Fabric performance is typically measured by the following methods:

1. Blower door air-pressure tests
Pressurised "blower door" testing is ideally carried out both during construction and on completion of a Passive House project in order to test its airtightness quality. However, as teams become more experienced, just one test should suffice in order to avoid unnecessary costs. This should be undertaken as soon as all of the airtightness measures have been completed. For Passive House certification, tests must be carried out by means of both a multi-point depressurisation and a multi-point pressurisation test, and the results averaged. Usually, UK air-testing results quote the lowest of either pressurisation or depressurisation, which can leave defects disguised. This practice is not acceptable in Passive House air testing.

The UK's first Passive House projects have consistently delivered excellent air-test results, over 15 times better than the UK Building Regulations standard for new buildings. This has been achieved in both new-build and retrofit Passive House projects. These results have been made possible by (1) intelligent planning of the line of airtightness at the design stage of every project, (2) communication of this to the construction team and (3) a collaborative approach to the practical achievement of this by means of on-site training and close site supervision.

The Princedale Road deep retrofit achieved $0.3h^{-1}$ @ 50Pa; Ranulf Road house is a new-build Passive House, achieving $0.44h^{-1}$ @ 50Pa; and the Mayville Centre is an example of a deep retrofit Passive House, achieving $0.42h^{-1}$ @ 50Pa. The Larch House in Ebbw Vale achieved $0.23h^{-1}$ @ 50Pa. All of these projects surpassed the Passive House requirement of $0.6h^{-1}$ @ 50Pa with mostly UK construction teams, none of whom had previous experience of building draught-free or Passive House buildings. The results that are consistently achieved in Passive House buildings indicate that a long-overdue and substantial improvement in Building Regulations requirements for building airtightness is deliverable.

2. Co-heating tests
A co-heating test is a method of measuring a building's whole heat loss or heat loss coefficient (in W/K). Co-heating tests undertaken by both the UCL Energy Institute and the Welsh School of Architecture on three domestic Passive House buildings in the UK found that actual performance is at least very close to, and often even better than, design estimates. This has been attributed to the accurate design measurement of the Passive House Planning Package (PHPP) and is in stark contrast to the general UK building stock, where tests carried out by Leeds Metropolitan University, UCL, BSRIA and the Usable Buildings Trust, amongst others, have shown a significant difference between design and as-measured thermal performance. For example, a co-heating test on a non-Passive House demonstration house to Code for Sustainable Homes Level 6, showed that it used more than 1.5 times the energy that it was designed to use.

3. Tracer gas tests
In all three Passive Houses tested by UCL and the Welsh School of Architecture, it was found that the tracer gas results, a method for analysing the airflow in buildings, complied closely with the blower door results.

4. In-situ U-Value heat flux measurements
Heat flux sensors can be used to measure the as-built U-values of different elements of the building fabric in order to check if this matches the designed U-values. As an example, the flux measured on the Ranulf Road house ground floor was 0.099 ± 0.013 W/(m²K), compared to a design target U-value of 0.103W/(m²K). In the same house, the flux was measured on a ground-floor wall. The measured figure was 0.097 ± 0.020 W/(m²K), compared to a design target U-value of 0.122W/(m²K). This provides evidence that the PHPP is quite accurate at predicted U-values.

5. Infrared thermography
Thermography surveys provide an opportunity to check for defects in the thermal performance of the as-built fabric. They can be used to find any areas of concentrated heat loss resulting from thermal bridges or air leakage. Analysis can be done externally and internally. A temperature differential is required between the internal and external environments, so it is ideal if the thermography survey can be completed in conjunction with the co-heating test.

Clockwise from above: typical equipment required for a coheating test; example of a roof-mounted weather station; carrying out a blower door test; carrying out heat flux measurements

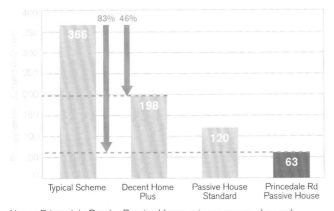

Above: Princedale Road – Passive House primary-energy demand compared to a typical building. (Primary-energy demand accounts for transmission losses. For example, primary-electricity demand in the UK, on average, amounts to 2.7 times the metered electricity.) Graph produced by Eight Associates for Paul Davis and Partners

Below: Thermal imaging at the Mayville Community Centre. Note the glass is reflecting heat from uninsulated flats behind the camera

6. Thermal bridge analysis

Thermal bridges can be avoided either by careful design, or by using one of the more than fifty building envelope systems that have been pre-calculated and certified for being completely free of harmful thermal bridging (see PHI home page). Cold bridging was absent in all the Passive House buildings investigated.

7. Scientific review of building systems

Careful design and commissioning should be carried out in consultation with the building occupants. This will tailor the building to the real needs of its users and avoid misunderstandings about its intended control methods. The factors that affect performance range from the control settings to opening windows and closing blinds. Research in this area can often be troublesome, disappointing and unrewarding. However, a method developed by the Usable Buildings Trust, called Soft Landings, tries to bring order to the process and reliability to the results. When Soft Landings and Passive House methods are embedded in the culture of the design team, they have been found to work together very well to discover and solve any initial faults and to achieve robust building performance.

In-use performance measurements

For the in-use monitoring of projects, sub-metering is required for electricity, gas, and hot- and cold-water utilities. Sub-metering enables design teams to provide a very good level of analytical aftercare for their clients. More advanced in-use monitoring can also be used to measure the efficiency of heat-recovery ventilation units and any air heating or traditional heating systems, as applicable. Internal temperatures, relative humidity and CO_2 levels can also be recorded to assess user comfort and health conditions. These can be analysed in conjunction with occupant surveys. Weather stations accurately record the external conditions – an important component of any in-depth monitoring.

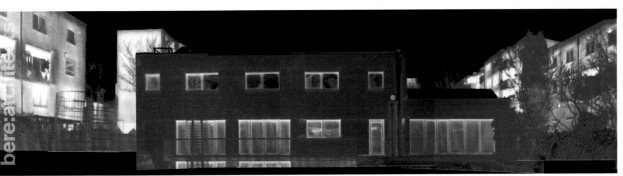

Monitored results – air quality (CO₂ & relative humidity)

In the Passive House at Ranulf Road, the first year of monitored data provided the following information on CO_2:

- The maximum CO_2 level in the master bedroom reached an occasional peak of <1,500 parts per million (ppm), keeping within the maximum indoor CO_2 concentration of 1,600ppm quoted by CIBSE Guide A, and 1,500ppm cited by the German DIN 1946 standard.
- In the living room, there were occasional peaks around 1,000ppm, well within recommended levels.
- The average CO_2 levels were excellent; 733ppm in the bedroom and 679ppm in the living room over the full year from October 2011 to September 2012.

In the same building, the average relative humidity (RH) range was 41.9–53.5%, indicating excellent internal conditions. The RH results that were measured in the house are optimal for human health because scientific research shows that RH of 40–60 supports the minimum of airborne fungal, bacterial and virus concentrations and a minimum of dust-mite particles, which are often blamed for causing asthma symptoms.

Optimal RH and CO_2 levels have been found in all of bere:architects' six different buildings that are being monitored with funding from the UK Technology Strategy Board. Even when special tests were conducted to measure the effect of daily indoor clothes drying, it was found that the Passive Houses avoided the moisture and mildew problems that occur in ordinary buildings. It was found that moisture is quickly removed in a Passive House building, in spite of long showers and clothes drying.

Monitored results – air quality (PM10 & PM2.5 particulates)

An independent air-quality report by Cranfield University (2013), funded by the UK Technology Strategy Board, comprehensively examined the air quality in the Passive House at Ranulf Road, London, and compared this with the air quality in a conventional house, also in Ranulf Road.

The report provides a comparison between the average level of harmful PM10 and PM2.5 particulates in the certified Passive House in London and the average level of PM10 and PM 2.5 particulates in the conventional house 100 metres along the same road. The average level of harmful PM 2.5 particulates inside the Passive House is half that of the conventional house.

It is also worth noting that the Passive House at Ranulf Road was found to have lower average indoor levels of harmful PM10 and PM2.5 particulates by a factor of three compared to the average level of particulates in the outside air.

Below: Indirect health effects of relative humidity in indoor environments from Environmental Health Perspectives, Vol. 65, p358. Sterling et al. 1986 (note optimum range extended into ranges of 30-40 and 60-70 to conform with general consensus)

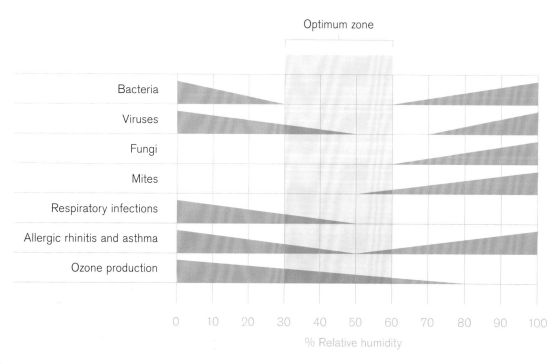

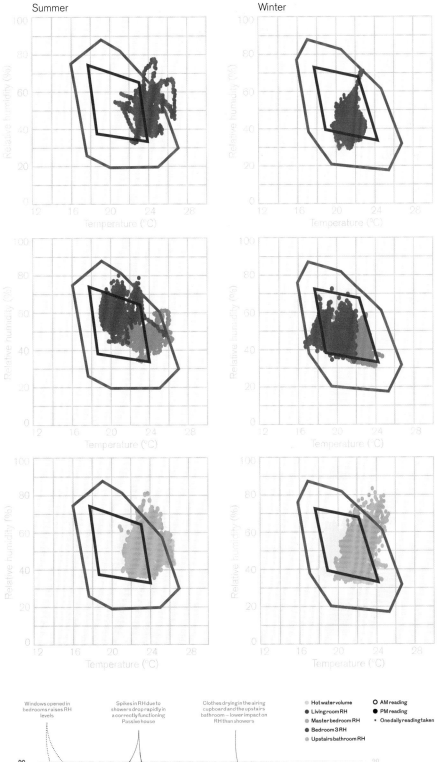

Summer   Winter

Comfortable
Very comfortable

● Hall   ● Living room
● Bedroom   ● Bedroom 1
● Living Room   Bedroom 2

Top two: Mayville Community Centre. Psychrometric charts for a typical summer month and period Dec 2012–Feb 2013. Conditions were optimal throughout winter. The average temperature of the main hall was 21.3°C. The basement has no heating and the average temperature in the coldest March for 40 years was 21.6°C, with the coldest Monday morning being 19.7°C.

Middle two: Ranulf Road Passive House. Psychrometric charts for Jun 2012 and Jan 2012. The higher summer living-room temperatures are due to the occupants' personal preference for enjoying the free warmth and their decision to override the blind controls, a point made by the occupants in the building user survey. The bedroom has perfect humidity and temperature in summer and winter months.

Bottom two: Passfield Drive retrofit (designed towards the Passive House standard). Psychrometric charts for May–Oct 2011 and Nov 2011–Feb 2012. The occupants enjoy winter warmth and choose temperatures that, in the living room, exceed 24°C, yet the overall energy saving in the first year of operation was over 50% compared to the pre-retrofit house.

Windows opened in bedrooms raises RH levels

Spikes in RH due to showers drop rapidly in a correctly functioning Passive house

Clothes drying in the airing cupboard and the upstairs bathroom – lower impact on RH than showers

● Hot water volume   ○ AM reading
● Living room RH   ● PM reading
● Master bedroom RH   * One daily reading taken
● Bedroom 3 RH
● Upstairs bathroom RH

Lime House Nov–Dec 2012
Graph of interior relative humidity (%RH). RH remained within optimum levels in all living spaces, rising briefly only in the two bathrooms after showers had been taken. Twice-daily clothes washing and drying had no discernible adverse effect on indoor humidity levels.

Overall energy use in Ranulf Road

According to Ian Ridley, UCL Energy Institute and RMIT University, Australia, the Passive House at Ranulf Road is one of the lowest-energy dwellings ever monitored in the UK, with a total gas and electricity consumption of $65kWh/m^2$ per annum, noting that so far only the terraced Passive House at Princedale Road by Paul Davis and Partners has been found to have a lower overall energy demand.

One of the Passive House requirements is that the specific space-heat demand of a building must not exceed $15kWh/m^2/yr$. At Ranulf Road, the measured specific space-heat demand in use during the first fully monitored 12-month period, July 2011 to July 2012 , was even better than designed at $12.2kWh/m^2/yr$. This is all the more remarkable because it was found that the occupants do not always interact with the building as expected or planned; for example the external solar blinds are often left down in the winter, reducing the useful solar gains, and also the indoor temperatures are set quite high in winter.

The results support the hypothesis that a Passive House building can accommodate varying types of user behaviour without seriously affecting building performance, which was, according to Dr. Feist, the intention during the development of the standard.

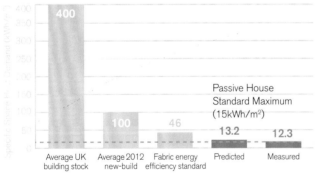

Ranulf Road Passive House specific space-heat demand compared with the UK existing housing stock and future best practice

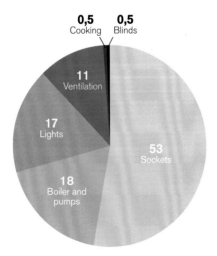

Ranulf Road Passive House, breakdown of electricity consumption by end use, February–July 2012

Overall energy use in the Mayville Centre

At the end of its first winter (2011), monitoring results found that the Mayville Centre made over 90% total energy savings compared to its pre-retrofit total energy use.

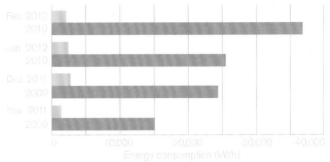

The Mayville Centre achieved over 90% reduction in overall energy consumption during its first winter of operation.

Analysis over the first year of occupation also shows that the centre performed significantly better than designed with regard to its specific heat load. This was due to higher occupancy than expected. In spite of the higher than expected occupancy, the overall primary-energy consumption was found to remain as designed.

The results show that PHPP is a robust tool for predicting in-use performance both for new-build and retrofit projects in the UK. We hope that these results will help convince sceptics that it is within their power to design buildings that can meaningfully, and reasonably robustly, contribute to increased energy efficiency and reduced CO_2 emissions – building efficiency that we are told by most scientists is essential and now urgently overdue.

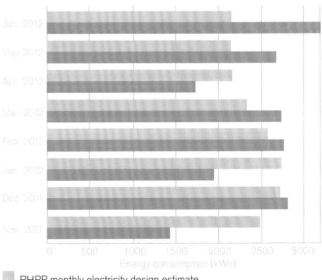

Mayville Community Centre Passive House retrofit – monitoring found that there is a good correlation between design expectations and performance.

Measuring occupant feedback

As a "reality check", Building Use Studies (BUS) were developed by the social scientist Adrian Leaman and the Usable Building Trust to give a quick but thorough way of obtaining professional-level feedback data on building performance, primarily from the occupants. Arup hold the licence to use the method, enabling them to authoritatively benchmark buildings against others on the BUS database. Ranulf Road, when subjected to a BUS, was found to have the highest user-satisfaction rating of any individual domestic building previously tested. Since only one occupant was surveyed, the result is clearly of limited significance; however, it should be noted that the occupant who was surveyed did not commission the dwelling or have any interest in low-energy buildings beyond the comfort and health benefits that she, as an asthma sufferer, would enjoy.

Overall energy use in social housing development at Wimbish

Monitoring work carried out for the Technology Strategy Board by the Adapt Low Carbon Group at the University of East Anglia has found that Parsons + Whittley's social housing at Wimbish for Hastoe Housing Association has achieved excellent comfort and energy performance results. Independent monitoring by the Adapt Low Carbon Group at the University of East Anglia has reported that the 6 flats and 8 houses at Wimbish have delivered over 80% reduction in gas use compared to the average domestic UK gas bill. One six-person household set aside £50/month for gas payments but their actual bill for 6 months (July – January) was £30.

Residents love their new homes and all residents have agreed that they would not want to go back to living in an ordinary house, reporting:

> "You just don't have the bills you would have in a normal house".

> "The houses are so light and spacious".

> "I'm happy putting my children's bunk beds by the window as there's no draughts, and the glass is not cold".

> "I'm less stressed. Having a lovely house we are proud of and look forward to coming home to is benefitting all of us".

> "You can put your furniture anywhere you want now" [no radiators].

BUS sample user comments

> "It's absolutely beautifully warm in here and zero degrees outside. And it's always got that lovely sort of ambiance in here. It feels really warm and comfortable and fresh."
> (Mayville Community Centre manager)

> "The house works in a very efficient manner because it requires very little heating even when it's subzero out there. So it proves that the Passive House concept works – in reality!"
> (Ranulf Road owner)

The owners of Ranulf Road have provided feedback that attests to the success of the underlying aim of the Passive House standard: to provide comfortable, healthy homes in an environmentally responsible manner for future generations.

Similar feedback has been provided at the Mayville Centre, the facility having been transformed from a cold building running with condensation and blighted by mould growth, draughts and other substandard indoor conditions, to a building that has optimal indoor comfort and optimal health conditions in winter and summer.

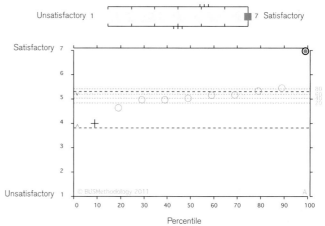

This sample data from the Building Use Survey (BUS) for the Passive House at Ranulf Road shows exceptionally high satisfaction with the air quality against benchmarks

Air quality and health

The DIN1946 regulation in Germany recommends that workstations should not exceed a CO_2 level of 1,500ppm, whereas regulations in England and Wales allow mean concentrations in schools of 1,500ppm averaged over the school day (DfES, 2006).

Research published by the City of Frankfurt in 2007 found that winter CO_2 levels in the air of classrooms in ordinary naturally ventilated schools in Frankfurt were for most of the time above 1,000ppm and a significant proportion of the time above 1,500ppm. These classrooms failed the German standard DIN1946.

The Frankfurt study also investigated the performance of a pilot Passive House school in the Riedberg area of the city. By contrast, the CO_2 levels in the pilot Passive House school always remained below 1,500ppm.

The Frankfurt study found that air quality in ordinary schools was poor because people were reluctant to open windows to obtain fresh air in winter due to cold draughts. So classroom CO_2 levels reached 1,800–2,500ppm before window opening occurred.

A Passive House building maintains healthy CO_2 levels, even during the winter, due to the heat-recovery ventilation system with carefully balanced supply and extract air flows. This "breathes" a constant stream of fresh air that is warmed by heat taken from air before it is vented from the building. In the warmer months windows are opened in a Passive House building without affecting its performance, just as in an ordinary building.

In the UK, Dr Tim Sharpe and others have highlighted the consequences of poor-quality ventilation in some low-energy buildings. There is plenty of evidence that certified Passive House buildings are not affected. Pages 36–37 add to this evidence, showing that perfect humidity levels are maintained even after indoor clothes drying. There is also some evidence that airborne concentrations of harmful particulates, which may cause lung cancer and asthma, may be reduced in Passive Houses.

Passive House buildings have a series of important design and commissioning requirements for ventilation systems that are missing from the UK Building Regulations. For example, the current Building Regulations make no requirement to design for pressure loss inside ducting. Ducting with high resistance will cause increased energy consumption and potentially inadequate air supply in some rooms while over-ventilating others, and poorly designed systems with high duct resistance create unnecessary noise pollution which may lead users to turn off systems. Furthermore, the UK regulations allow primitive "trickle ventilation" gaps in window frames and they permit crude bathroom extractor fans that waste heat and create cold draughts.

Passive House design and commissioning techniques for ventilation systems offer an excellent model for improvement of the UK Building Regulations.

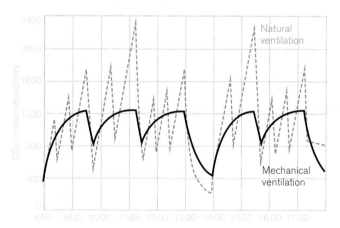

Graph compares CO_2 concentration in a mechanically ventilated classroom (max spikes of 1,200ppm) with CO_2 concentration in a naturally ventilated class room (max spikes 2,300ppm). Research published by the City of Frankfurt, 2007

The importance of skills

This is where the main challenge to Passive House delivery lies – and the main opportunity. The nurturing of skills is synonymous with investment in them, which in turn is synonymous with investment in people.

Skills of the architect

Employing an architect is one of the ways of achieving the best value for a site. Their imagination enables architects to visualise what others often cannot see. Few purely technical people can provide the imaginative leaps that an architect can.

In the hands of an architect who can generate good design ideas as well as high-performance buildings, both short-term and long-term value can be created. This is obviously very attractive to clients, which may be one reason that there appears to be a growing interest in Passive House amongst design-led architects.

Skills to plan a Passive House project

Passive House training courses are provided by the Passivhaus Institut (PHI) in Darmstadt. Normally these courses are held in German, but once a year if there is sufficient interest, the PHI holds a 10-day intensive course in English. Training courses accredited by the PHI are also delivered by partners across Europe, including the UK.

However there is no better way to learn than immersing yourself in the International Passive House Conference every year. English speakers are looked after with excellent simultaneous translation, and the talks are usually of a very high quality. A text book (supplied in English) provides abstracts of all the presentations, laid out according to scientific conventions. It's impossible to attend three or four lectures being delivered simultaneously in different halls, and the text book makes fascinating reading and gives the opportunity for broadening your research.

There is also an excellent exhibition linked to the Passive House Conference. It is always a mad dash to try to get around the exhibition when you are being pulled in all directions, not least of all by people you may not have seen for a year. Scientists from the PHI provide group tours around the exhibition on the first day, and these are always enlightening and keep you abreast of the world's leading low-energy and ecological developments. Regional conferences are also worth attending. The UK holds a stimulating annual conference run by the UK Passivhaus Trust and the BRE.

My third tip would be to just buy the software, which is sold at a very low, not-for-profit price that usually surprises people. Then, just dive in and learn. Yes, the learning curve is steep but the manual helps avoid too much frustration. A new book is planned for publication in 2014 which will help guide people in using the PHPP for their first Passive House Projects. It will be written by my co-director Sarah Lewis and published by RIBA Publications. There is also an excellent text book by Janet Cotterell and Adam Dadeby, and in 2013 Robert McLeod and Christina Hopfe will also publish a technical manual.

Skills to deliver a Passive House project

Good-quality contractors seem to relish the opportunity to do a job well and be appreciated for that. This makes them very receptive to, and respectful of, a knowledgeable architect with the new Passive House skills. Yes, any learning curve requires effort and some sacrifice at the outset. However, it is a well-known fact that practice brings rewards. We are working with traditional contractors who are steadily building skills within their workforce. By retaining those skills, either by means of direct-labour staff or of partnering companies, these contractors are becoming very competitive. Those who have a thirst for embedding skills within their organisation are the contractors who will thrive as the statutory building codes are tightened.

What skills am I referring to? A critical skill is achieving airtight construction, and organising a project design and programme to facilitate this. But this will not be achieved without cooperation between architect and contractor. In particular I would refer to thoughtful and knowledgeable design for airtightness that makes it possible for a contractor to achieve the stringent targets. This means that the architect must enable, by design, every logical step in achieving airtightness, for some designs will hinder airtightness and some will facilitate it. More detailed information on this topic can be found in the publication Airtightness Report; practical guidance to achieve excellent levels of airtightness in Passivhaus building fabric. This is published by bere:architects and available free of charge as a download from the Research page of the bere:architects website: www.bere.co.uk/research.

Case Studies

Passive House is relatively new in the UK and Ireland, with the UK's first certified buildings completing in 2009 and 2010. In a few short years, Passive House is already recognised as a supreme method to achieve high-performance buildings and to reduce carbon emissions – and nobody would deny that the UK needs much better buildings. But for these buildings to have the greatest impact, they need to be beautiful examples of design – either traditional or contemporary – in order to encourage more architects and building owners to choose Passive House for mainstream, affordable, comfortable and healthy solutions. This means that they need to be architect designed.

This chapter is primarily an analysis of case studies from around the world, but it starts with a short review of some of the UK's first Passive Houses.

In 2009, John Williamson – who combines the skills of qualified architect, services engineer and carpenter – delivered the first building in the UK to be certified as a Passive House. The local authority training offices, Canolfan Hyddgen, in Machynlleth, mid-Wales was closely followed by a domestic Passive House project, also in Wales. The Canolfan Hyddgen office building won the New Build Project of the Year in the highly respected CIBSE Building Performance Awards 2011 given by the UK's Chartered Institution of Building Services Engineers.

Introduction

The case studies contained in this book are all certified Passive House buildings selected for the convincing illustrations that they present. A few buildings that I would have liked to include were not fully certified. An example of this is a beautiful little house on Rhode Island, US, designed by Zero Energy Design architects. I almost included the house anyway because it is so encouraging that such a beautifully straightforward little house can also be a Passive House. It has all the spirit of a pioneer New England house to me. Other pioneer projects in the end could not be included because, while in many senses key projects, particularly in the UK context, they lacked the necessary photographic images.

In 2010, several further Passive House certified projects were completed. They are:

- Denby Dale Passivhaus, built using traditional masonry construction by Bill Butcher and the Green Building Store with Derrie O'Sullivan, architect
- The Centre for Disability Studies in Essex by Andrew Simmonds
- 4 Ranulf Road, a timber-framed dwelling in London by bere:architects
- Larch House and Lime House, timber-framed affordable-housing prototypes in Wales by bere:architects
- Underhill House, an earth-bermed masonry construction by Helen Seymour-Smith
- Hadlow College Rural Regeneration Centre by Eurobuild

In 2011 and 2012, further Passive House schools, office buildings and "Retrofit for the Future" projects were completed.

The Princedale Road project by Paul Davis and Partners was the UK's first domestic full Passive House retrofit. It also incorporated an exciting new development: a UK manufactured Passive House window suitable for historic buildings and approved by conservation planning officers.

In 2011, a 28-unit residential bungalow development was completed by the Gentoo Group at Houghton-le-Spring, near Sunderland according to designs by Mark Siddall, then of Devereux Architects. Twenty five of the bungalows are certified Passive House dwellings built to look like traditional bungalows. However, for their Passive House reincarnation their redundant chimneys have been given a delightful new 21st-century purpose – to suck in fresh air rather than belch out noxious, polluting gases! This was one of the first projects to test Passive House solutions in the UK at the scale of terraces.

Also in 2011, a development of 14 certified Passive House homes was built by Hastoe Housing at Wimbish in Essex to designs by Parsons + Whittley architects at close to the build cost of ordinary social housing. As well as being concerned about the health, wellbeing and comfort of their tenants, Hastoe also want to give their tenants the best possible opportunity to pay their bills in the long run – including their rent. With average household energy costs probably reduced to just a few hundred pounds a year, Hastoe are forthright in their view that renting Passive House homes is a factor in their sustainable business plan.

Similar motivations were behind Orbit Housing's desire to build 18 flats and five houses at Sampson Close, Coventry. For their first Passive House project, the timber-frame wall and roof panels were manufactured in Germany. Other pioneer UK projects include Viking House offices, Dover; Nash Terrace, Aubert Park, London; Interserve offices; Oakmeadow Primary School and Bushbury School; the Totnes Passivhaus Retrofit by Janet Cotterell and Adam Dadeby and the Mayville Community Centre retrofit.

Architype completed two primary schools in 2012 which are said to achieve Passive House certification without additional cost, thus sweeping aside the only real impediment to the uptake of the standard for all new schools in the UK. One of these schools, Bushbury, is featured as a case study. Architype's uptake of Passive House has been swift and comprehensive, and they are now one of Britain's most prolific Passive House practices.

Grove Cottage, designed by Simmonds Mills Architects, is the first Passive House Enerphit retrofit in the UK. The Enerphit standard helps achieve significant energy savings in existing buildings, while recognising that affordable retrofits may not easily achieve the full Passive House standard. Elliott Drive, Coventry, by ID Partnership for Orbit Heart of England, is the second Passive House Enerphit retrofit in the UK. The adjoining building was designed to a lesser quality and Orbit's intention is to compare the performance of the two houses, albeit with different residents with their own particular habits.

There are numerous other exciting projects completing in 2013 and 2014 in the UK, and at the same time a number of design-led and mainstream architectural firms are being asked to incorporate the Passive House approach in some larger projects. Camden Council's Chester Balmore Housing by Rick Mather Architects will be completed in 2013, not without challenges for the design-and-build team that includes Architype. Cartwright Pickard, who first made headlines with their Murray Grove prefabricated housing scheme in London, are in 2012–13 attempting their first Passive House residential block: Sulgrave Gardens in London for Octavia Housing. Sergison Bates architects are also designing their first Passive House, the delightful "Tower House" on a rural site in the south of England and the ecological pioneers, Gaia architects, recently completed a house in the hills of the Scottish Borders. Tobias Schaffrin, an ex-David Chipperfield architect, is also building his first Passive House development in London. It is hoped that some of these projects will feature in a future edition of this book.

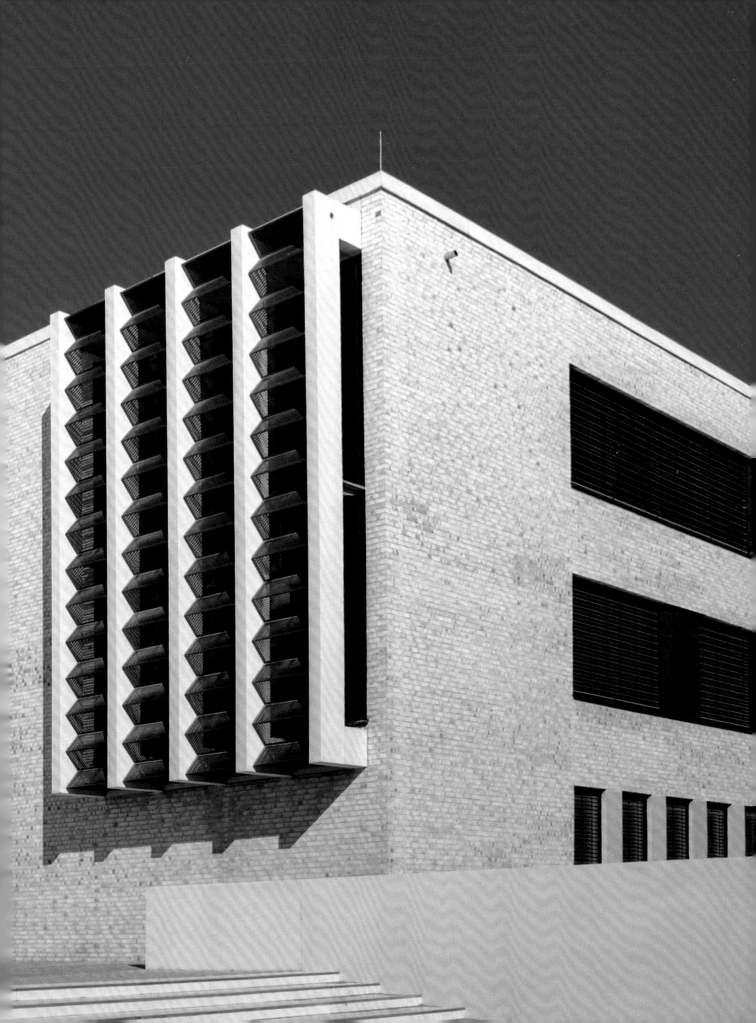

Background

The competition for the Riedberg Grammar School was held in summer 2009, five years after completion of the City of Frankfurt's successful pilot Passive House primary school in nearby Kalbacher Höhe, also in Riedberg.

Ackermann + Raff won the competition for a new grammar school for 1,350 pupils in autumn 2009. Construction was started in November 2010. I saw the school as the building was completing in April 2013. It's a masterpiece in brick, in which architecture triumphs over technical constraints.

Brief

The brief was to create a pioneering school concept – a cultural centre to serve the community, rather than just an institution for learning; it called for spatial and atmospheric qualities, as well as for flexible use. Corridors of classrooms were taboo – instead, each of the eight school years was to be defined by its own central court.

The design

The Dutch architect Aldo van Eyck declared "the city must be like a large house" and conversely "a house must be like a small city". Inspired by this thought, the architects organised the building as a series of internal volumes and external courtyards, connected by a series of long, straight "roads". The building appears deliberately non-hierarchical; movement through this learning landscape, this microcosm of a city, is richly articulated by a chequerboard layout of internal courts or "living rooms" and outdoor spaces. These present a subliminal message about the linking of public and private space in an open-school concept, and the modulation of the manmade and the artificial by natural light and shade.

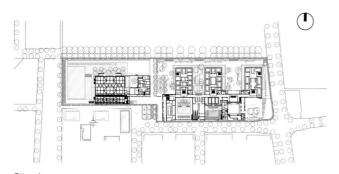

Site plan

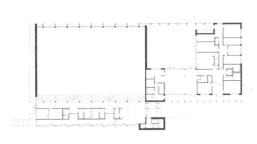

Ground-floor plan

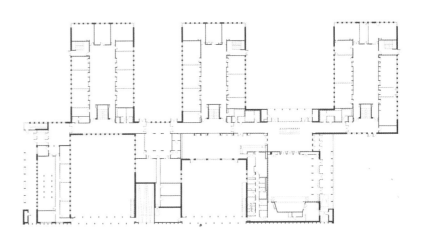

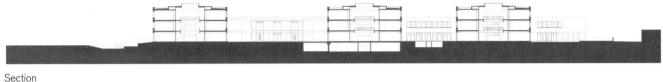

Section

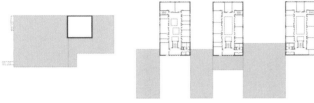

Second-floor plan

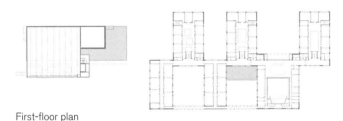

First-floor plan

Location	Friedrich-Dessauer-Straße, Frankfurt-Riedberg, Germany
Date	2013
Client	Hessen Agentur GmbH (City Development Agency)
Owner	City of Frankfurt – Department of Education
Team	Architect: Ackermann + Raff GmbH Construction Management: Gassmann + Grossmann GmbH Services engineer: CSZ Ingenieurconsult GmbH Structural engineer: Bollinger und Grohmann Ingenieure Passive House consultant: Passivhaus Institut Electrical planners: Raible + Partner GmbH Building physics: Ebök GmbH Fire protection: Endress Ingenieurgesellschaft GmbH Landscape architects: Pfrommer + Roeder
Energy	15.0kWh/m²/yr specific space-heating demand (predicted)
Air test	0.27h⁻¹ (50Pa pressure difference)

The facades are made from a smooth, almost white brick that creates a subtly textured surface. Sometimes colonnaded with white precast concrete elements, they have an almost classical elegance. The building has a concrete frame and uses traditional masonry materials, while the design embraces the idea that the future can be contemporary, elegant and entirely compatible with the ecological imperatives of our time.

All of the City of Frankfurt's public buildings have for some years been built to the Passive House standard. This is mature Passive House design, in which the Passivhaus Institut helped the design team overcome a number of technical challenges without compromising the architectural vision. The resulting technical strategies for user and environment are fully integrated and appear subordinate to the architectural concept.

Evaluation

The concrete ground slab is insulated from above, which means that the brick facades can rest directly on to the stepped concrete edge beam. This results in a novel approach to avoiding cold bridging of the concrete columns. Internally, 1,200mm x 240mm thick columns reduce to just 340mm x 240mm as they pass through 250mm of insulation on top of the ground slab. The approach to structure and thermal isolation shows how Passive House can accommodate a strongly driven architectural vision so long as any sub-optimal thermal detailing is compensated for in other respects to maintain the essential energy criteria. A total of 280mm of insulation is used in the walls, and 300–600mm of insulation is used in the roof, which is presumably where the payback occurs.

Air is distributed horizontally at roof level, then dropped via short vertical risers, freeing the ground floor entirely of air ducts. Heat and ventilation are decoupled. Presence detection is used to control the ventilation, without CO_2 sensors. The supply-energy demand can thereby be reduced by 80% in low occupancy. Extract air is at constant volume. The controls are simple and robust, the only compromise being that ventilation hours will be extended by just one person in the building. Summer ventilation is passive stack with motorised facade and roof vents, which double as smoke vents in the event of fire.

Background

This three-family apartment building was Switzerland's first Minergie-P-ECO multi-family home and the winner of the 1st Passive House Architecture Awards, PHI 2010. Minergie is a Swiss sustainability label for buildings that offer higher performance than the country's statutory requirements. For this project, the "P" corresponds to the Passive House standard, and the "ECO" designation adds ecological requirements such as daylight use, indoor air quality and noise emissions.

Brief

The architect, being a member of the private building owners' association, had a strong influence on the design approach. Besides providing contemporary living spaces for flexible use, the focus was to develop a sustainable architecture with a high living environment. Re-densification was considered by the three families to be an important aspect of sustainable living.

The design

The building site was a challenging triangular plot, previously occupied by seven garages. The new building forms a transition between two very different urban geometries, aligning itself with both. The entrance facade lies parallel with the adjacent footpath, while the timber-framed south-west elevation is parallel to the planning grid of the nearby 1950s villas. So while uncompromisingly contemporary in its design, the building is also arguably quite contextual in terms of volume and typology.

The resulting slender plan and large surface-to-area relationship nevertheless result in a building that achieves great comfort and very low energy consumption.

Existing garages were demolished and relocated into a basement beneath the house, which extends under the garden. Above the basement, a three-storey staircase and service core provides structural stability and is wrapped by a timber frame which is glazed to the south-west in order to optimise the provision of daylight. Facing the path to the north-east, the timber frame is vapour-diffusing and clad with cementitious wood fibreboard with minimal fenestration.

Site plan

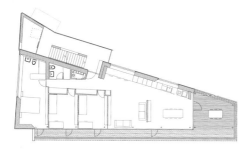

Upper-floor plan

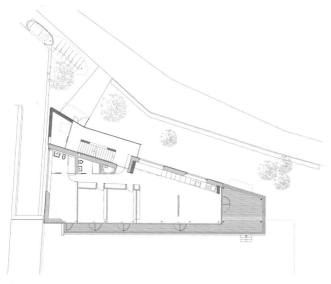

Ground-floor plan

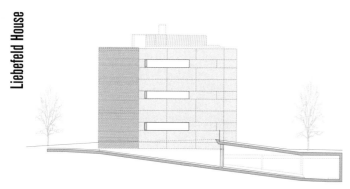

Cross section

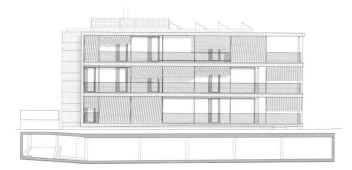

Long elevation

Location	Gebhartstrasse, Liebefeld, Switzerland
Date	2006
Client	Private building owners' association
Team	Architect: Halle 58 Architekten GmbH Services engineer: Enterprises Riedo Clima Structural engineer: Tschopp + Kohler Ingenieure GmbH Timber structure planning: Hrb Ingenieurbüro für Holzbau Energy, building physics and acoustics: Gartenmann Engineering AG Contractor: Beer Holbau AG Ventilation, heating: Rideo Clima AG Windows: Jakob Stoller
Energy	15.3kWh/m²/yr specific space-heating demand (predicted)
Air test	0.6h⁻¹ (50Pa pressure difference)

The glazed south-west facade is shaded by a deep terrace on each floor, and opens on to a galleried balcony with external wooden roller blinds for summer shading. Even when the blinds are closed, the space between the windows and the blinds creates a delightful feeling of openness.

The building includes a number of shared spaces: the roof is planted and provides a communal garden space for the residents, and the basement contains a shared washing machine and a music room.

Renewable energy technologies were integrated:solar thermal panels provide heat for domestic hot water and a low-temperature underfloor heating system, while a wood-pellet boiler provides backup in the winter months.

Building to the Minergie-P-ECO standard requires that the architecture is conceived as a whole building system. The large area of glazing gives excellent daylight levels at the same time as providing an effective means of harvesting solar gains on a bright winter afternoon. The proportion of external surface area (739m²) to treated floor area (408m²) is high, and needs to be compensated for by a very high quality of fabric in order to limit heat losses. To reduce thermal bridges to a minimum, the concrete storey of the building – the basement – is only accessible from the outside by an external staircase. This helped ensure that the whole vapour-diffusing timber construction could be airtight.

Careful attention was applied to the detailing of the large areas of glazing. Most of the windows are fixed, to assist airtightness and to reduce the potential for heat losses from window frames. The result is glazed-facade U-values of between 0.65 and 0.92 W/(m²K), with the triple-glazed units achieving 0.5 W/m²K.

As part of the search for a balance between solar gain and solar shading, some thermal mass was added to the timber floor structure in the form of cement screed which contains low-temperature floor heating pipes.

Thanks to natural and untreated building materials, together with heat-recovery ventilation, the quality of the indoor air is reported to be very high.

Evaluation

This project is a fine example of integrated design; maintaining architectural quality without compromising technical excellence or energy efficiency. The available funds have been used wisely to procure a long-lasting and high-quality small apartment block with high sustainability credentials. Despite its high specification, the building was economical to build, is economical to run, and has been designed so that room layouts are adaptable to meet future requirements. The result is an excellent synthesis of beauty and ecology.

Background

Ludesch is a municipality in Vorarlberg with approximately 3,000 inhabitants and a long tradition of ecological awareness. In 1994, the local council decided to join the International Climate Alliance of European Cities with Indigenous Rainforest Peoples. In 1995, the energy efficiency of the local building fabric was assessed; based on this assessment, a programme of locally funded energy incentives was launched in 1997. In 1998, Ludesch became a member of Vorarlberg's "e5-Program", which is a regional initiative for the qualification and certification of energy-efficient municipalities.

The 3,135m^2 Ludesch Community Centre project is an exemplary building for Europe, and has received national and international awards. It is distinctive in the way its planning and development have been rigorously integrated into what, perhaps, is the finest example of an ecologically designed Passive House building anywhere in the developed world. Excellent fitness for purpose; inclusive design; the multifunctional use of space; integration into its urban context; the use of local raw materials and manufacturing; the elimination of toxic materials and pollutants, including silicone, solvents, formaldehyde, softeners, fluorocarbons and PVC – all this forms a thorough and holistic approach to sustainability (biology, ecology and energy efficiency). This building is sustainable in the sense of dealing economically with limited resources such as land and energy, through sensible deployment of ecological and "sound" building materials. The project also had to be implemented within normal cost limits despite involving additional, ecologically motivated investment.

Site plan

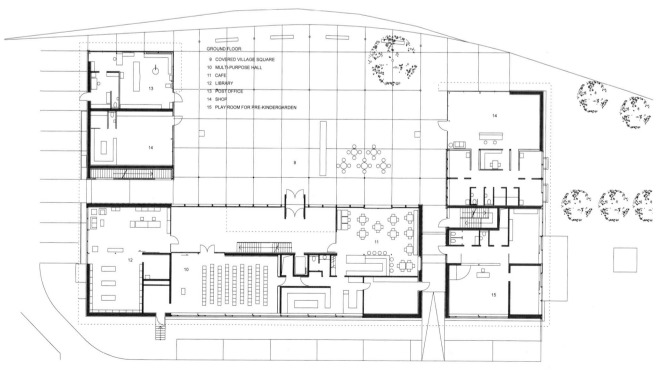

GROUND FLOOR:
9   COVERED VILLAGE SQUARE
10 MULTI-PURPOSE HALL
11 CAFE
12 LIBRARY
13 POST OFFICE
14 SHOP
15 PLAY ROOM FOR PRE-KINDERGARDEN

Ground-floor plan

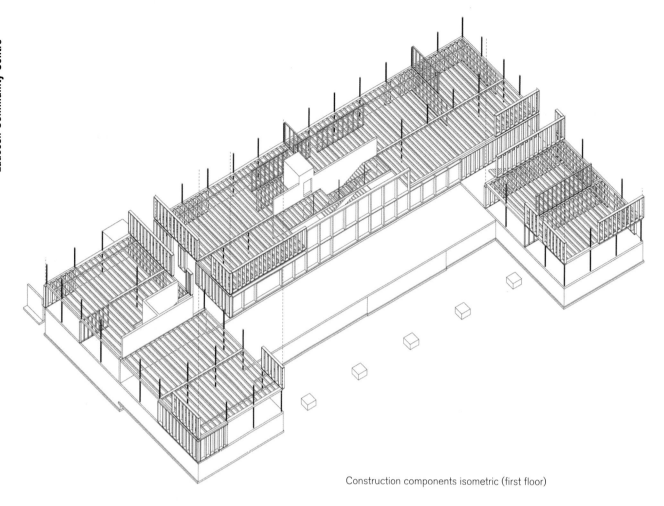

Construction components isometric (first floor)

Brief

It was decided to build a new community centre in 1995. In 2000, Hermann Kaufmann's office was appointed. The aim was to establish a centre that would act as an ecological prototype – at a reasonable cost and with the participation of the local residents.

The design

Ludesch is a linear village that needed a focus. It had neither a concentrated centre nor a traditional village square. The community centre comprises three volumes that enclose and define a public forecourt with a glass canopy that opens to the north-west, facing the village road.

The ground level features a post office, a shop, a large foyer, a library, a cafe, a hall for 100 people, a physiotherapy practice and a day nursery; the upper floor houses offices, seminar rooms, archives, a computer centre and a sanitary area; the basement, with rehearsal and club rooms, connects the three wings of the complex. The roof features cantilevered timber "string courses", which protect the untreated wood facades, doors and glazing from the weather. Cable-mounted solar blinds shade the windows. The use of locally grown, untreated, knot-free silver fir, used on all surfaces from walls to furniture, creates a harmonious indoor atmosphere with visual, acoustic and sensual qualities.

The two-story timber construction was erected over a reinforced concrete basement. Walls and ceilings are prefabricated box beams. The silver fir is rough-sawn, wire-brushed or smoothly planed according to application; the dark-oiled oak flooring is a pleasant contrast to the light fir walls and ceilings.

The exterior walls were insulated with cellulose, while sheep's wool was used for the wall linings and the partitions. Sheep's wool also replaced the commonly used polyurethane window insulation. This detail came at an additional cost of only €800, and averted the oft-occurring, rash-forming allergic reactions suffered by some window technicians during assembly.

Solid timber walls stiffen the structure, and slender steel columns were used where slimmer profiles were desired. Locally produced silver fir was used instead of oriented strand board (OSB) for the structural sheathing, which represented a 30% reduction of the environmental impact. The wooden structural elements were prefabricated by two local companies. Concrete anchors, screws and adhesive tapes were used for assembly in place of glued connections. Care was taken to avoid the use of substances that could affect the health of the indoor environment. One result was the development of PVC-free sealing strips, now part of a standard product range. Each of the project's 214 products was carefully assessed for its material composition and ecological quality.

In addition to its operational energy efficiency, the primary-energy consumption of the construction process (embodied energy) was reduced by 50% compared to that of "standard" Passive Houses. It was further intended to halve the ecological footprint of the building envelope compared to conventional architecture. This refers (a) to the global warming potential (GWP) of construction materials, which compares the effect of a specific substance to that of the same mass of carbon dioxide in order to determined how much it contributes to global warming, and (b) the acidification potential (AP) of substances and materials compared to sulphur dioxide: the atmospheric oxidation of sulphur dioxide in the presence of water produces sulphuric acid, which then falls to earth as acid rain, causing acidification of water bodies and soils, with well-known negative impacts on flora and fauna.

Further environmental indicators describe the percentage of non-renewable primary energy in construction materials, the percentage of volatile carbon compounds and the formaldehyde content produced during the construction of thermal building envelopes. These values are calculated based on the standards and methods set out by the Austrian Institute for Healthy and Ecological Building.

Evaluation

The centre's specific heat demand is 13.8kWh/m^2/yr. The ventilation system is connected to a groundwater pump and can supply the rooms with preheated or precooled fresh air. Hot water is generated by 30m^2 of solar panels on the roof. Additional heat energy is supplied by the biomass district heating plant. While the built volume of the community centre equals that of approximately 22 single-family homes, it only uses as much energy for heating or cooling as two conventional detached houses. Four zones are each equipped with a separate ventilation system to improve energy efficiency. The supply air is tempered to a maximum of 22°C. A humidifier is integrated into the ventilation unit.

The translucent PV panels generate 16,000kWh of electricity each year. The power generated is fed into the grid, and supplies electricity to five households.

This iconic building demonstrates the future of construction in a more responsible world. The Ludesch Community Centre is as meticulous in construction as it is in planning. It demonstrates a goal that we can aspire to: beautiful, comfortable buildings, healthy for the environment and healthy for the individual, produced almost entirely of locally grown materials and local manufacturing. I have visited this building several times since I first saw it at the 2007 Bregenz International Passive House Conference, and my admiration grows with every visit.

A tour

Ludesch Community Centre is connected to the St Gerold Community Centre (see page 82) by a fabulous mountain route that includes another very beautiful low-energy community centre by Hermann Kaufmann's brother Johannes. The tour is described on page 86.

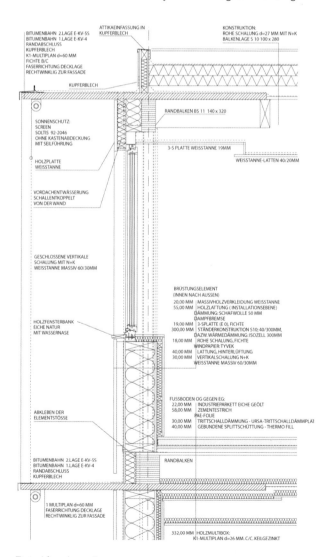

Typical facade section

Location	Raiffeisenstrasse, Ludesch, Austria
Date	2005
Client	Gemeinde Ludesch (Municipality of Ludesch)
Team	Architect: Hermann Kaufmann Cost consultant: Norbert Kaufmann Mechanical services engineer: Synergy Consulting & Engineering Structural engineer: Mader & Flatz Ecology/biology consultant: Institute für Baubiologie Contractor: Jäger Bau Ventilation, heating: Lippuner Energie- und Metallbautechnik Windows: MGT Mayer Glastechnik
Energy	13.8kWh/m^2/yr specific space-heating demand (predicted) Energy used in construction was calculated to be 50% of that used with traditional methods Greenhouse potential of construction: one third of traditional methods
Air test	0.48h^{-1} (50Pa pressure difference)

Kamakura House

Background

There is currently no minimum energy-efficiency requirement for new residential buildings in Japan, where one million new houses are built every year. A dwelling with single-glazed windows and no insulation is still acceptable.

This low-cost 78m^2 house is Japan's first Passive House and has been designed to be strong enough to resist earthquakes and termites. With an outstanding air-test result of 0.14h^{-1} @ 50Pa, it has clearly been built to a very high standard. The architects of this prototype dwelling were closely supported by building physicists from the Passivhaus Institut and the completed building provides evidence that a Passive House can offer excellent comfort in a warm and humid summer climate where the energy needed for dehumidification is as high as that required for cooling.

Brief

KEY ARCHITECTS were approached in 2008 by the client, who wanted to build an ecological family home. He was very open to the proposal to build a Passive House, despite the fact that an energy-efficient building of this kind had not yet been built in Japan. The client had only one "absolute-must" requirement: that the house be driven solely by electricity, as its mortgage was provided by the owner's employer, an electric-power company.

The design

The design is deliberately simple; a two-storey family unit, which in spite of its contemporary design fits harmoniously into the mature neighbourhood, including some traditional Japanese wooden buildings.

Inside the entrance to the house is a traditional lowered area for taking off shoes in the Japanese tradition. A corridor leads to the bathroom, the master bedroom and the children's room which is designed to be divided once the two children of the family are older and need more privacy. A staircase leads up to the open-plan living-dining area at first-floor level. The carefully located windows frame pleasant views over the river and the hills of Kamakura. Because of the high land prices and the resulting small plot size, the site was not big enough to provide private open space at ground-floor level. To overcome this, the architects designed an alternating-tread staircase that leads to the roof and gives the family an area of private open space and a viewing platform to overlook the city.

As a significant part of the client's mortgage went into buying the site, the building itself had to be designed to a very tight budget. The house was built using a 140mm-thick timber frame supported by a simple insulated concrete raft. The frame is insulated with 140mm wood fibre and over-clad by a further 100mm of wood-fibre insulation batts. The windows are triple-glazed wood–

Site plan

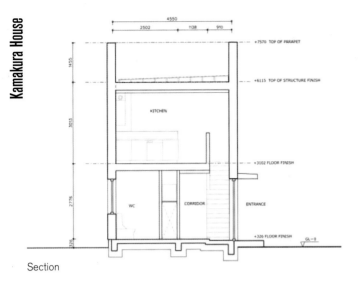

Section

First-floor plan

Ground-floor plan

aluminum units, which had to be shipped from Germany as this quality of window was not yet produced in Japan. Cedar cladding was scorched to preserve it against rot and the risk of fire, according to the local tradition. This very traditional Japanese building material is unfortunately in decline because of modern fire regulations.

Evaluation

In such a humid subtropical climate, reducing the dehumidification and cooling demand during summer is more difficult than reducing heating demand in winter. Careful detailing was required in order to avoid the risk of condensation within the external walls during both summer and winter months. Another difficult issue was the strict earthquake requirements for Japan, which require a rigid loadbearing wall. This building project is being treated as a pilot project by the Passivhaus Institut in Darmstadt, and monitoring of its performance will help improve the Passive House calculation methods for warmer regions.

Location	Kamakura, Kanagawa, Japan
Date	2009
Client	Taro Hasumi
Team	Architect: KEY ARCHITECTS Services engineer: Ecomo Passive House consultant: the Passivhaus Institut Contractor: Kenchikusya
Energy	15.0kWh/m²/yr specific space-heating demand (predicted)
Air test	0.14h⁻¹ (50Pa pressure difference)

Liebig Gym

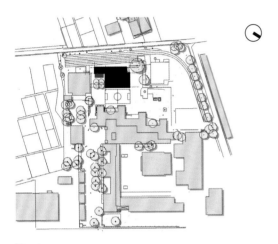

Site plan

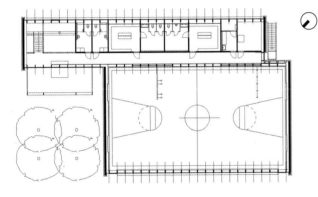

First-floor plan

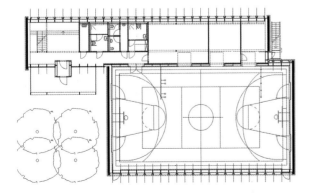

Ground-floor plan

Background

The competition to develop a modular Passive House gymnasium system to replace 26 old-fashioned elementary-school gymnasiums in Frankfurt was won by D'Inka Scheible Hoffmann Architects in 2007.

I saw the Liebig School gymn on a tour at the International Passive House Conference in April 2013 and was strongly impressed by the beauty and coherence of the design, resulting from a meticulous and almost virtuous approach to detailing – in which the development of a timber system has been elevated to a work of art. This is no accident. It is the result of the City of Frankfurt's investment in excellent, architect-led design, and the intelligence of the brief in recognising that children feel the influences of their environment very directly and intensely; responding well to natural, breathing and non-polluting buildings.

By contrast I cannot help reflecting on the system in the UK, where all too often we procure contractor-led, soul-crushing buildings that express the triumph of a go-getting society over the precious gift of providing enduring quality.

I feel sure that the results of the high-quality design that is strongly evident in Liebig can only have a positive effect upon the generations of children who will use this building and the 26 other gymns in the replacement programme.

Brief

Recognising the potential to achieve huge energy savings and maintenance-cost reductions from a carefully planned programme to replace Frankfurt's substandard elementary-school gymns, the City's Office of Education opted for a high-quality, architect-led, system-design approach.

The first two prototypes were to start in autumn 2008, and finished a year later. Two more gymns were completed in autumn 2010, a further four in 2011 and two more will be completed in 2013/14.

The design

The building reflects in scale, composition and volume the particular site structure and urban context, as well as the requirements of a gymnasium.

The system comprises three elements: the sports hall, the serving spaces, and a covered entrance area or pergola. These three elements can be arranged in different ways in response to the urban context.

The system is constructed from KERTO columns (360mm x 75mm) and beams (750mm x 75mm) supported by a concrete floor slab. KERTO is an engineered wood product, made from 3mm rotary-peeled spruce veneers glued together to form a homogeneous beam that achieves great strength with relatively slender sections. The use of timber also facilitates design that is free of thermal bridges.

Liebig Gym

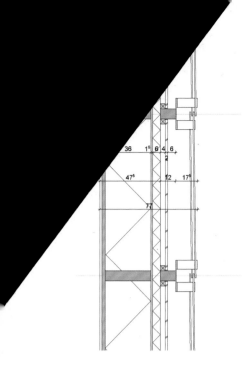

Facade detail (plan)

To give the structure the mandatory 30 minutes' fire protection, the KERTO columns are, where exposed, clad on their sides by 21mm-thick, three-layer engineered board from Finnforest Merk. This is also used as the finished wall surface throughout. The three-layer board has carefully chamfered arrises. Small gaps between the boards and bands of panel containing perforations provide acoustic dampening. Airtightness is achieved behind this by structural OSB board.

Evaluation

The beauty of the main hall and its ancilliary spaces, the wonderful quality of the light and the refined wood engineering all contribute to make gentle, warm, tactile and acoustically excellent interiors that are ingeniously clad in glass which is juxtaposed with reassuringly robust and austere brick exteriors. This is an uplifting and at the same time intimate building for children to practise sport in, and also to inspire and nurture them.

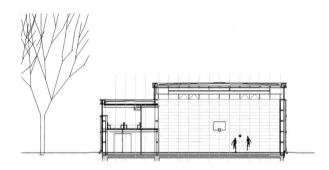

Cross-section

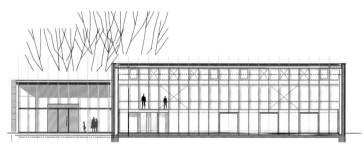

Long section

Location	Kollwithstrasse, Frankfurt, Germany
Date	2011
Client	Municipal Corporation of the City of Frankfurt
Team	Architect: D'Inka Scheible Hoffmann Architects BDA Mechanical services engineer: inPlan Ingenieurbüro Structural engineer: Dr. Mühlschwein Ingenieure Gmbh Electrical engineer: IPlan Farnung Building physics: Passivhaus Dienstleistungs GmbH Fire prevention: BPK Concrete work: Fa. Adolf Lupp GmbH Masonry: Universal-Putz GmbH Timber work: Fa. Müller Holzbau GmbH Facade/glazing: Kuhn + Dörr Fensterbau
Energy	15.0kWh/m²/yr specific space-heating demand (predicted)
Air test	0.25h⁻¹ (50Pa pressure difference)

Ranulf Road House

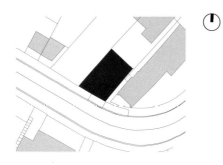

Site plan

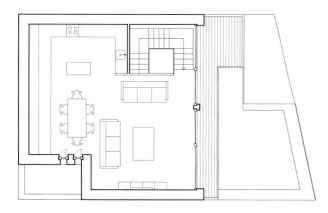

First-floor plan

Ground-floor plan

Background

This two-bedroom house was London's first certified Passive House. It resulted from an 18-month collaborative research project, during which time bere:architects employed a timber-framing technician from Austria.

In common with other Passive Houses, it uses principles of building physics that are designed to ensure that the fabric of the building remains dry. This enables the building superstructure to be built with timber that has no chemical treatment.

Brief

The client wanted to build a healthy, two-bedroom "eco-house" for their daughter, who suffers from asthma, after hearing that the very healthy indoor conditions of a Passive House might help relieve her symptoms.

The design

The small site faces south, and large windows fill the house with light. It's an "upside down house", which means that the bedrooms and bathrooms are on the ground floor and the open-plan living room enjoys the first-floor light and views. It was originally designed with natural wood ceilings together with a solid staircase balustrade, and classic Arne Jacobsen bathroom and kitchen fittings. However, the client decided upon a palette of bold white plastered ceilings, a glass staircase balustrade and contemporary, white bathroom fittings. The family dog, Twinkle, is also white, completing the design coordination of every detail.

Large triple-glazed, draught-free windows eliminate outdoor sounds and flood the rooms with daylight. Even on an overcast day, solar radiation helps to warm the house in winter, due to special glass properties.

External, retractable, metal louvre blinds help to keep the building cool in summer, and can be adjusted to create a feeling of privacy without blocking the views. Clerestory windows over the first-floor kitchen bring south light into the back of the large room and give a glimpse of the biodiverse wildflower meadow on the roof. Small windows at the back of the house are particularly effective at ground-floor level, bringing light borrowed from a tiny private courtyard into the second bedroom. Such details create a welcome sense of space in a tight urban location.

The walls are timber-framed, which saves space, and the inner layer of insulation is made from natural wood fibre. Structural floors are made from massive interlocking cross-laminated timber planks with three layers of wood-fibre insulation beneath the floorboards. This virtually eliminates the transmission of any footfall sound between floors, and gives the house a feeling of solid quality.

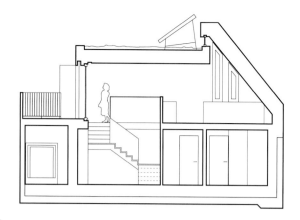

Section

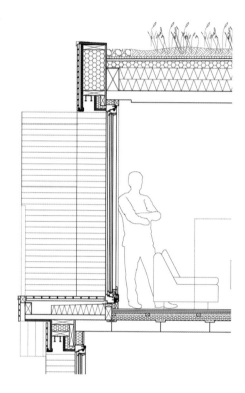

Detail

The heat-recovery ventilation unit is integrated within the bicycle shed by the entrance, in order to maximise indoor storage space. The location of the ventilation unit makes it ideal for testing a new long-life filter system. The filter is designed in such a way that it can be changed from outside under a maintenance contract, a feature that could become standard practice with both private and rental-sector housing. Hot water is supplied by a solar compact heater unit, which has a tiny backup boiler to top up the hot water and also provide a little heat to rooms, when required, by means of a gentle flow of pre-warmed fresh air.

Evaluation

The building has been monitored by University College London (UCL) with funding from the UK Technology Strategy Board. It has been found to be performing slightly better than designed, and even though it has no radiators or underfloor heating the occupants are very comfortable in winter and summer.

The house maintains perfect indoor humidity levels, and the high quality of construction has guaranteed a complete absence of condensation. Indoor air-quality testing was carried out by Cranfield University in March 2013 during a cold-weather period. The focus of the investigations was to measure amounts of volatile organic compounds (VOCs) including formaldehyde, particles, nitrogen dioxide and radon in the air. Residents were content with the indoor air quality and none of the compounds quantified exceeded available indoor air-quality guidelines. Indoor levels of harmful PM10 and PM2.5 particulates were found to be three times less than outdoor levels on the particular day, and up to four times less than a conventional house in the same street that was measured on the same day.

Ranulf Road House illustrates how it is possible to comfortably meet the UK's planned 2016 zero-carbon compliance standard. This reassuring fact should be welcomed by politicians and contractors. Set in the heart of the UK's design-conscious capital city, it is hoped that this building will deliver what is needed to help develop a low-energy revolution in the UK.

Location	Ranulf Road House, Camden, London, UK
Date	2010
Client	Private
Team	Architect: bere:architects Services consultant: Alan Clarke Heat-recovery ventilation design: Green Building Store Structural engineer: Rodrigues Associates Superstructure engineering and fabrication: Kaufmann Cost consultant: Richard Whidborne PHPP calculations: bere:architects Green roof specialist: Dusty Gedge Contractor: Visco
Energy	13.7kWh/m²/yr specific space-heating demand (predicted) 12.1kWh/m²/yr (actual)
Air test	0.44h⁻¹ (50Pa pressure difference)

Background

Bushbury Hill is located in a deprived area of Wolverhampton, West Midlands, yet the completed building provides arguably one of the best environments for primary-school learning anywhere in the UK. It has been built for the same cost as an ordinary school, yet it is warm, comfortable, full of daylight and draught-free. The plan and section work together to create a series of delightful and uplifting, well-ventilated spaces that are filled with daylight.

Brief

The brief was for a standard one-form entry primary school (210 children), plus a 30-place nursery and facilities for a local "Multi Agency Support Team". A critical requirement was to engage in a thorough consultation process in order to develop a solution that met the educational needs and expressed the ethos of the school in its efforts to provide high-quality education for children from the tough surrounding estates. During early consultation sessions, the client agreed to set the environmental target to achieve Passive House certification so long as the standard available budget and tight timescale were not exceeded.

The design

To achieve the rigorous technical demands of Passive House within a standard budget required the early integration of Passive House design, informing and influencing every decision about form, design and detailing. At the same time, the design team retained a relentless focus on simplifying and optimising the scheme.

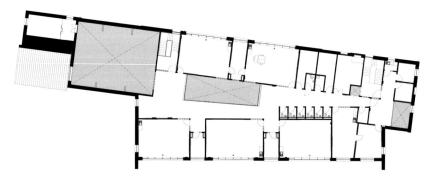

First-floor plan

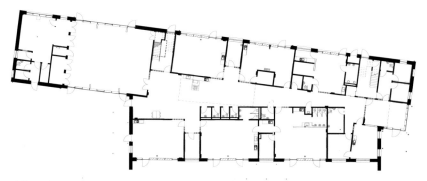

Ground-floor plan

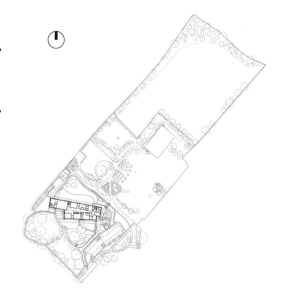

Site plan

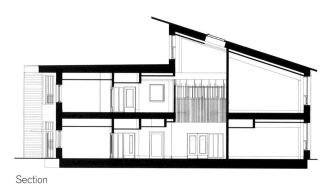

Section

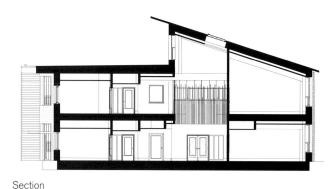

Section

Location	Old Fallings Lane, Wolverhampton, UK
Date	2011
Client	Wolverhampton City Council
Team	Architect: Architype Services engineer: E3 Consulting Engineers Structural engineer: Price & Myers Passive House consultant: Elemental Solutions Contractor: Thomas Vale
Energy	15.0kWh/m²/yr specific space-heating demand (predicted)
Air test	0.53h⁻¹ (50Pa pressure difference)

Architype's construction approach was to use a prefabricated, lightweight, well-insulated timber frame with a loadbearing stud wall, wrapped by an additional layer of insulation, created by non-loadbearing I-beams.

Ground conditions dictated piled foundations, but to avoid thermal bridging the building sits on a concrete slab which floats over insulation that thermally isolates it from the ground beams and piles.

External cladding uses locally sourced brick and UK-grown timber. The triple-glazed windows have composite timber/ aluminium frames.

Architype are well known for their rigorous ecological approach to sustainable and non-toxic materials. The use of certified timber is a fundamental part of their sustainability strategy. Indeed, the material is used in every aspect of the construction, including external and internal walls, intermediate floors, roofs, glulam columns and large-span beams, and cladding. Other internal materials and finishes were specified with high sustainability credentials, such as natural organic linoleum, non-toxic mineral paints, organic stains, and rubber barrier matting made from recycled tyres.

The services strategy includes heat-recovery ventilation for winter operation, together with passive ventilation for summer days and night cooling. External brises-soleil have been incorporated on the south facade, providing protection against overheating during hot summer days.

Clerestory windows bring an abundance of daylight into the central hub space and help light the rear of classrooms. They also form part of the summer ventilation strategy, creating an escape route for warm, used air drawn out from the classrooms through integrated wall vents.

Evaluation

Architype have successfully produced two of the UK's first certified Passive House schools. Their energy consumption is being rigorously monitored, and the electrical circuits have been sub-metered. The indications are that they are meeting the Passive House targets.

British Standards require sprinkler water to be kept at 10°C, and maintaining this accounts for an extraordinary 25% of all electricity used by the school. To reduce this in future school projects, Architype will build mini Passive House enclosures around the sprinkler tank.

The kitchen hob is electric-induction which avoids excess heat and reduces ventilation requirements. The design team is providing a two-year "soft landings" support service to assist the users in learning to operate their building so that it provides them with the greatest enjoyment, comfort and energy efficiency. The head teacher and the pupils love their new school, and praise its design for its comfort in both winter and summer and for its plentiful fresh air.

St Gerold Community Centre

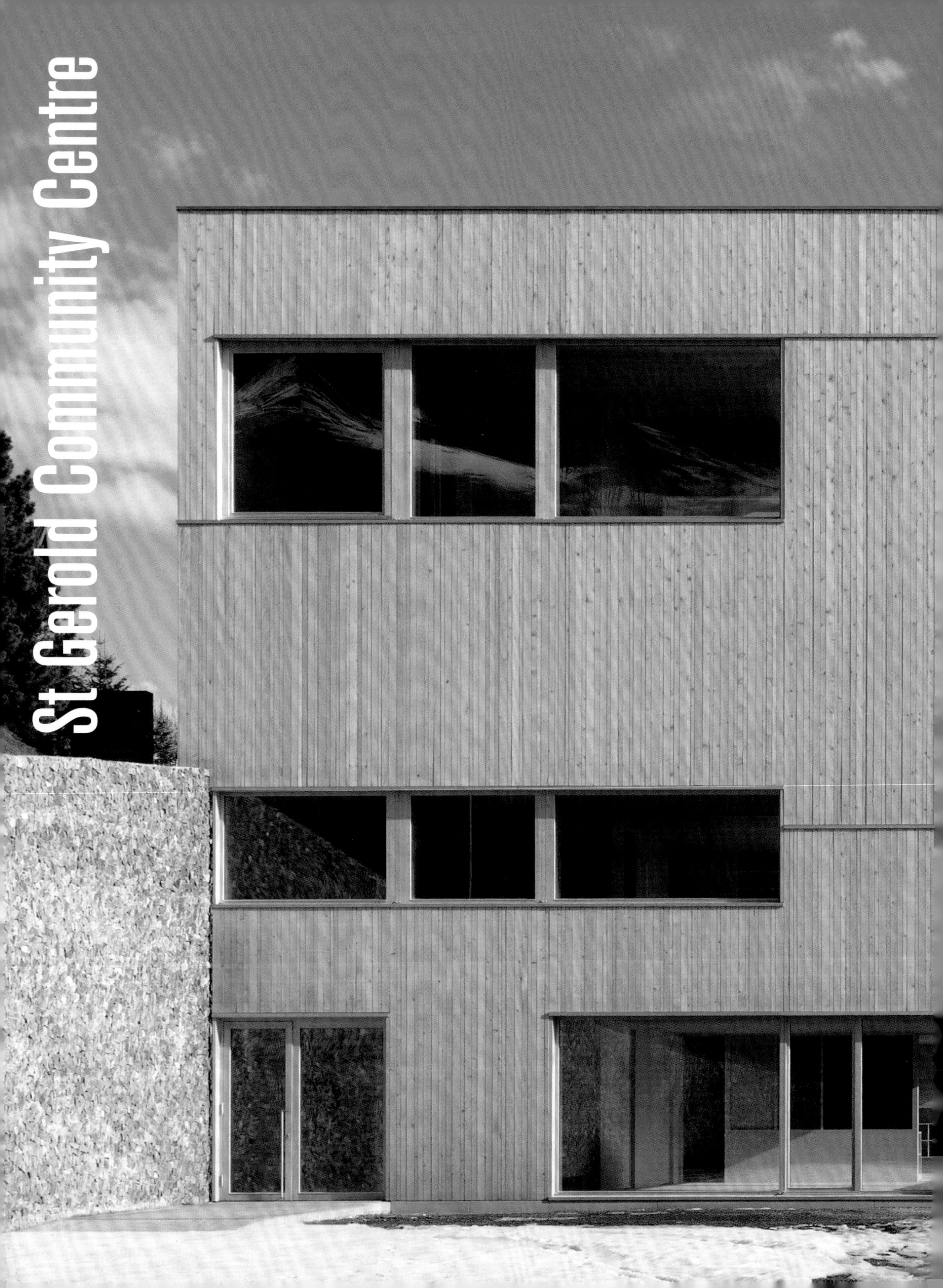

Background

This is another of my favourite fabulous Vorarlberg buildings. Situated alongside the mountain road, the building is characterised by a strong but simple geometry and the playful use of horizontal lines that serve to define the length of the vertical wood-cladding strips. The landscaping in front of the building is executed in cor-ten steel and is equally simple, beautiful and refined, reminding one of the work of Carlo Scarpa. The building uses high-quality, slow-growing mountain softwood throughout. The timber used inside the building is almost entirely knot-free – which lifts it out of the ordinary, helping to create a sense of immense refinement. The Vorarlberg carpenters have an extraordinary pride in the quality of their work in solid timber, and their skills are displayed in this building by simple, highly refined cabinetry made from raw wood that is smooth to the touch – but you can still feel the grain, which has been enriched from mechanical soft-brushing of the untreated surface of the wood. By contrast, the floors are rough-finished to provide a durable, non-slip surface.

Brief

The new community centre contains a kindergarten, a children's game club, a village shop, a multipurpose room and municipal offices. The community wanted the building to be as near self-sufficient as possible, to be ecological, sustainable and to utilise as far as possible locally grown materials and local manufacturing.

The design

The setting of the St Gerold Community Centre is characterised by steep slopes, and the site provides beautiful southerly views of the landscape and mountains.

The community centre appears to be two storeys high from the road but it is in fact a four-storey building, with the kindergarten at the lower side of the slope opening on to a quiet garden hidden from the highway. The building retains both of the original level surfaces of the landscape (the village square to the street as well as the playground below) and places itself as a connecting element between them. The functions of the new centre are stacked vertically over its four floors, with the relatively low-ceilinged kindergarten at the base and the busy shop and public spaces at road level.

The complex functional connections are brought together inside by simple spatial devices and construction elements. Precisely positioned window openings offer carefully chosen views that enhance the experience of moving through the building.

The community centre is designed as a timber building, constructed directly off a reinforced concrete base. This was the first four-storey timber building in Vorarlberg. All construction units of the building are formed from cross-laminated timber and come mainly from local, municipal forests. The wood is all completely untreated.

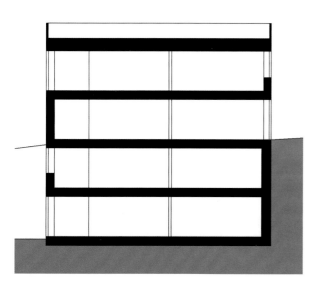

Site plan

Section

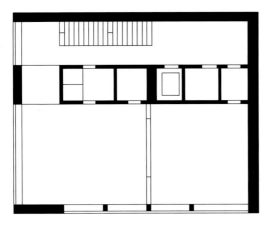

Second-floor plan

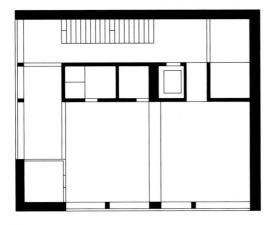

First-floor plan

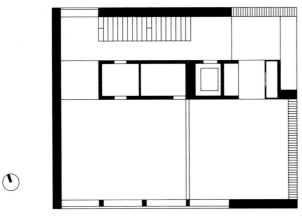

Ground-floor plan

Location	Faschinastrasse., St Gerold, Austria
Date	2008
Client	St Gerold Municipality Property Management Department
Team	Architect: Cukrowicz Nachbaur Architekten Services engineer: Werner Cukrowicz Structural engineer: M + G Engineers Passive House consultant: Ing. Angelika Rettenbacher
Energy	10.7kWh/m²/yr specific space-heating demand (predicted)
Air test	0.44h⁻¹ (50Pa pressure difference)

Evaluation

The compact volume of the building is designed to function efficiently as a Passive House, and it is said to be nearly self-sufficient although no data is available at the point of writing. Nevertheless the building is already considered an exemplar with respect to ecology, sustainability and the creation of "local value".

A tour

St Gerold is located towards the end of one of the loveliest mountain routes that I know. Starting off at Hermann Kaufmann's Ludesch Community Centre (see earlier case study), I recommend travelling up the side of the mountain in the direction of Raggal. There you will find a wonderful low-energy community centre designed by Hermann's younger brother Johannes Kaufmann. It's located above the road near the beautiful historic village church.

Then continue down the mountain, crossing to the other side of the valley and climb towards Blons and St Gerold until you find Cucrowicz Nachbaur's St Gerold community centre perched facing south across the valley.

Afterwards, visit Hermann Kaufmann's riding school and other agricultural buildings directly below at the end of a tiny private road that leads to the extraordinary Benedictine Monastery of St Gerold.

Finally, to round off a beautiful trip, travel on to Thüringerberg, visit the Biosphärenpark building (take a look at the back of the building for a pleasant surprise) and time your visit for a meal in the beautifully intimate Gasthaus Sonne next door. The views are spectacular and you will be refreshed by wholesome, locally grown food served with a smile.

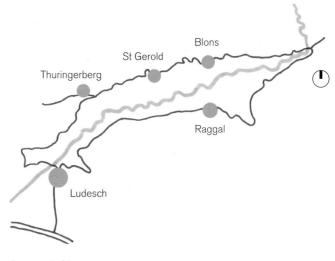

A suggested tour

Langenpreising Kindergarten

Background

The village of Langenpreising is located on the Bavarian gravel plain at the edge of the Alpine region and close to Munich. Set amidst fertile agricultural land, it provides an attractive living environment, closely connected to nature. In the last two decades Langenpreising's population has been gently growing, and in 2009 it decided to expand its facilities for children. The community wanted an energy-efficient building and selected Gernot Vallentin, who is one of Germany's most experienced and creative Passive House architects.

Brief

The client and funding body was the community of Langenpreising. In spite of a tight budget, the community were clear that they wanted an environmentally responsible building, both in terms of its energy use and in its use of local products and services with low embodied energy. It was also a requirement that the kindergarten would connect to the combined heat and power unit that already served the other community buildings, including an elementary school, a gymnasium and a church kindergarten.

The design

The new school forms part of a small cluster of educational buildings grouped around a village green and looking across open farmland. On approaching the building, the sculptural side elevation is glimpsed between mature chestnut trees. It appears to hover delightfully like a sculptural tree house on the western side of the village green while its garden elevation is optimally orientated towards the south.

The building has two levels: the garden level and the "hovering" storey. The garden level comprises a meandering wall with iridescent colouring intended to accentuate the surrounding trees and shrubs, and contains the outdoor space and a tool shed. The wall continues inside where it separates the entrance from the more private, contained classroom spaces.

The tree-house element provides a welcoming shelter for the ground-floor entrance, and on the garden side it contains a south-facing balcony which also forms a loggia for the ground floor beneath. The effect of playfulness is enhanced by timber cladding of irregular widths, together with the strong larch columns in the loggia, and the sculptural, outdoor staircase.

Site plan

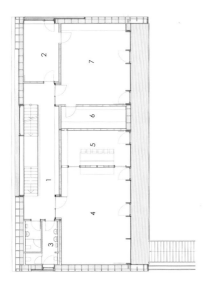

First-floor plan

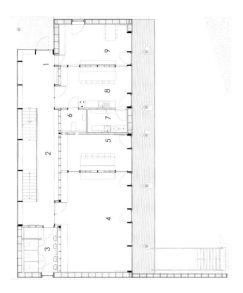

Ground-floor plan

Evaluation

Gernot Vallentin's priority was to achieve affordability in conjunction with the Passive House standard. This was achieved by careful planning and optimisation of the construction and detailing of the building. Prefabricated timber framing was used with raw finishes. The first-floor balcony and staircase act as a fire escape. This also simplifies the fire-protection strategy, since the enhanced escape route means that fire separation is not needed, allowing the money-saving use of cascade ventilation between floors. The balcony and projecting roof also act as a summer sun-shield for the ground and first floors, so that internal blinds provide sufficient additional shading. All these factors in turn helped keep costs at an affordable level and enabled non-specialist local suppliers to bid for work.

This building is a "declared passive house". In operation, both the comfort and the heating consumption satisfy the requirements of the Passive House standard.

The children love the verandas and balconies, which show how intermediate spaces can play a very important role in creating an enjoyable and interactive building. Langenpreising offcrs an inspiring example of a how to create a very beautiful, playful but cost-effective kindergarten building that promises to nurture and support the work and imaginative play of children for generations to come – and "just happens" also to be a Passive House.

Location	Zehentweg, Langenpreising, Germany
Date	2010
Client	Commune D -Langenpreising
Team	Architect: ArchitekturWerkstatt Vallentin Services engineer: Ingenieurbüro ITG Structural engineer: IB Jochum Passive House consultant: ArchitekturWerkstatt Vallentin Contractor (timber): Josef Lackner
Energy	15 kWh/m²/yr specific space-heating demand (predicted)
Air test	0.28h⁻¹ (50Pa pressure difference)

Gasser Bau Offices

Background
The construction company L Gasser & Co. AG decided to move its headquarters to its own production yard outside Zurich, to improve internal communications and to reduce travel distances for employees.

The robust appearance of the building rearticulates the company's image, and its bold siting resolves the spatial geometry of the site. Being elevated and bridging between two massive piers, the new offices create a space beneath with protection from the elements, allowing vehicles to be moved around and providing storage space for materials.

Brief

The architects were asked to embody the company's history, work ethic and its values in a long-lasting modern office building. The new structure – with offices for management, administration and construction supervisors – was to fulfil the Minergie-P standard.

The Gasser group's own Passive House planner was involved in the process from the beginning, and the energy design was executed without compromising the organisation, appearance and structure of the building.

The design
The shape of the building was optimised in collaboration with both the structural and civil engineers. All loads are concentrated within only two pylons, to reduce penetrations in the thermal mantle to a minimum. The main structure is completely wrapped by an insulated perimeter "jacket".

The building volume is divided into three main areas: administration and conference spaces to the east, workstations to the west and a core zone in between.

The concrete surfaces are exposed internally, which is aesthetically pleasing and at the same time provides thermal mass to moderate the internal climate. So the concrete has a major influence on the indoor character and atmosphere of the building. It is used in different ways and with varying textures – some of it was poured on site and some was industrially prefabricated to create contrasting, smooth ceiling elements. Perfectly finished surfaces deliberately contrast with and accentuate the imprecise imprints of formwork panels, which in turn become a metaphor representing the beauty of the carpenter's craft; a durable casting of the "handwriting" of his work.

As buffer storage, the huge building mass ensures perfectly even temperatures in both summer and winter. Air circulates freely within the almost five-metre-high spaces, and this is assisted by the fact that none of the separating walls – loadbearing or partition – reach the ceiling.

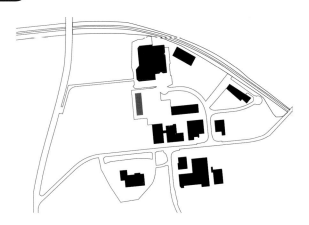

Site plan

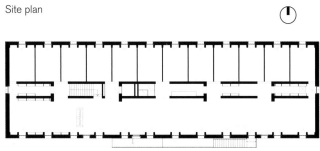

First-floor plan

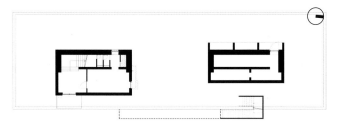

Ground-floor plan

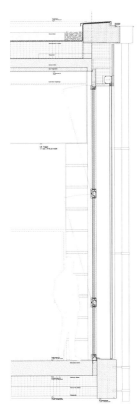

Facade detail (section)

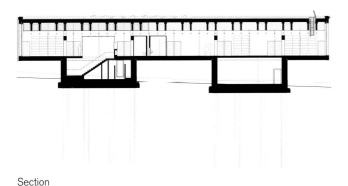

Section

The internal space creates the same sense of calm that one feels when entering an agricultural storage shed. The ventilation outlets are located – like house martins' nests in a barn – high up on the walls. The services strategy is rational and expressed with visual clarity. For ease of maintenance, all technical equipment is easily accessible. Ducts are routed from the central plant room, which is located in the ground floor of one of the podiums. Since all services run via the core, the external walls of the building are free from any technical installation – and the resulting simplicity reduces the risk of breaching the line of airtightness.

A two-layer shading system regulates the heat gains from the outside. "Intelligent" outdoor blinds prevent the interior from overheating in summer. If solar gain is desired, internal curtains allow individual shading to be adjusted for each workstation.

Evaluation
A construction firm's new office building on its own production yard creates a new space with an expressive concrete architecture.

Prefabricated, fair-faced concrete elements were fitted with precision. Joint sizes were minimised to ensure that the building is airtight. The concrete forms the line of airtightness, and joint gaps were sealed carefully to achieve the required level of airtightness.

The facade is an elegant, everlasting rain skin of slightly corrugated ceramic tiles with rear ventilation. The tiles protect the external insulation, which is up to 320mm thick. Precise planning prevented the need to cut any of the tiles.

At roof level, local vegetation grows directly in the topsoil that was taken from the area covered by the building. Rainwater is mainly stored here, and no additional watering is necessary. If heavy rain occurs, excess water is discharged by traditional-style gargoyles to seep into the ground beneath. The planted roof design was developed as a research project with the Zurich University of Applied Sciences.

Location	Rütisbergstrasse, Oberhasli, Zurich, Switzerland
Date	2011
Client	Gasser Bau AG
Team	Architect: Käferstein & Meister Architekten Services engineer: Grünberg Partner Structural engineer: Lüchinger+Meyer Bauingenieure Passive House consultant: Gasser Passivhaustechnik Contractor: L Gasser & Co. Ventilation, heating: D&W Aerosmart X2 with GSHP
Energy	17.5 kWh/m²/yr specific space-heating demand
Air test	0.4h⁻¹ (50Pa pressure difference)

Molkereistrasse Residence

Background
This subsidised student housing was designed by **be** baumschlager eberle for the Vienna hou sing association, MIGRA.

Brief
The building was required to house 278 Austrian Exchange Service students in a contemporary, functional and very low-energy building.

The design
The Molkereistrasse Passive House residence is a seven-storey block containing 133 apartments with a total of 280 rooms. Commissioned by a non-profit housing provider, this low-cost student housing saves the building operator €40,000 per year in energy costs compared to one built to the normal building code, and reduces carbon emissions by approximately 100 tonnes a year. The result shows how, in the hands of a talented designer, low-cost housing can be full of delightful surprises for the building user and contribute positively to the urban environment at the same time. At Molkereistrasse, all this is achieved in a restrained, elegant and appropriate way.

Externally the building uses a simple and economical palette of white render and 320mm-thick EPS (expanded polystyrene) insulation over reinforced concrete walls. The facade is enlivened by external sliding shutters made from copper (specified at a time when the material was relatively cheap to buy). Each occupant is able to slide their bedroom shutter by simply opening their tall, tilt-and-turn bedroom window and reaching out over the glass balustrade.

By closing a shutter on the street facade, the occupant reveals a delightful, gentle, verdigris-coloured panel where the shutter stood when open. The complementary colour works so well because it is a perfect match with the hue of naturally patinated copper.

Internally, the corridor spaces are naturally lit by shafts of light from above, a clever yet simple device that was intended to poetically echo the effect of pools of light falling upon a meandering forest path. In fact, the light enters through roof glazing and descends the height of the building via fireproof glass floor panels in the corridors.

The students live in modular units, which range in size from a single-room apartment to a four-room flat. Parquet floors and white walls create the appearance of a hotel. The cooperative living arrangements are hinted at by the occasional glimpse of student kitchenettes with glazed windows linking them to the corridors.

A heat-recovery ventilation system is mounted on the roof. Over the doorways of rooms are mounted mini-radiators, supplied by district heating to top up the temperatures when required.

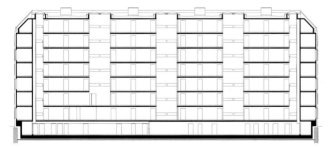

Site plan

Long section

Evaluation

A post-occupancy evaluation was carried out by Dr Martin Treberspurg of the Vienna University of Natural Resources and Life Sciences. It was found that with such a tiny heat demand and free, thermostatically controlled heat supply, students kept their rooms at a median temperature of 23.24°C. When the measured energy data of the 10,500m² building is converted to standard conditions (20°C), the building was found to perform according to design with a total primary-energy consumption of 115kWh/m²/yr. As expected, the total energy required for showers is far higher than the heat energy needed to maintain a very high level of comfort.

Heat-energy consumption is very slightly higher than planned (16.6kWh/m²/yr), but the difference is negligible and this is still extremely good – the more so since it was found that some of the students were frequently leaving their windows open in the tilt position in winter, rather than lowering their room-temperature thermostat. In anticipation of this, and to reduce the wasted heat, the room's heating is automatically switched off if a window is opened. In a user survey of 26 dormitories, 83% of respondents felt this was a good idea and 84% of users were completely satisfied with their apartment.

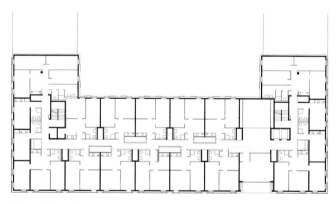

First-floor plan

Ground-floor plan

Location	Molkereistrasse, Vienna, Austria
Date	2005
Client	MIGRA (non-profit housing association)
Team	Architect: **be** baumschlager eberle Services engineer: team gmi Structural engineer: Vasko+Partner Ingenieure Cost consultant: ARWAG Passive House consultant: Vasko+Partner Ingenieure
Energy	12.0kWh/m²/yr specific space-heating demand (calculated) 16.6kWh/m²/yr (actual)
Air test	0.49h⁻¹ (50Pa pressure difference)

Hudson House

Background

Otherwise known as the Hudson Passive Project, this is the first Passive House to be built and certified in the state of New York. Located on a three-hectare plot in the heart of the Hudson Valley 160km north of New York City, the house is approximately 150m² in area. Inspired by the simple forms of some of the historic rural structures in the area, this poetic and sensitively designed house has generous warmth of character. Inside, graceful bow-arch beams of southern pine, 7.5m high at their apexes, frame an open, loft-like plan. A seven metre tall, south-facing wall of glass at one end lends this "traditional" home a distinctly contemporary feel. The arrangement of the plans is also very tidy, with almost no wasted circulation space.

Brief

The Hudson House began as a self-funded research and development project to achieve the highest energy conservation without the use of alternative energy technologies. The importance of the project was recognised when it won a grant from the New York State Energy Research and Development Authority to enlarge the design team to include building scientists and mechanical engineers. Finally, this pioneering project was adopted by a regional builder to pursue as a speculative project, in order to demonstrate the skills of his construction team.

The design

The design of the Hudson House was primarily driven by the goal of achieving the highest possible energy-conservation levels using only passive systems. The smaller the building, the harder it is to achieve high scores using passive systems because there is such a low ratio of interior volume to exterior surface area. Additionally, tall spaces in small buildings can sometimes add to this difficulty. The shape of the house and the location of its fenestration were carefully calibrated using the Passive House Planning Package in order to offset these disadvantages; however, it took numerous design iterations to reach the point at which the desired performance looked achievable.

The Hudson House was designed to be a demonstration house as well as a speculative development project. The house has been open for tours, and all the data and methods of construction have been generously shared with the industry through an ongoing series of lectures and presentations. It is hoped that the experience of visiting a Passive House will convince visitors of the sense of this approach. Such visits leave people inspired and feeling very positive towards Passive House concepts.

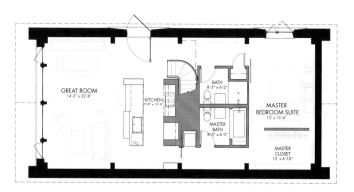

First-floor plan

Ground-floor plan

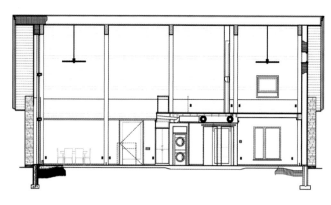

Section

Evaluation

All the Passive House criteria have been met in the Hudson House, and the "fabric-first" approach, with its excellent levels of insulation has given the homeowner the ability to make a 90% reduction in energy consumption for heating and cooling. As always, an important factor in the dramatic reduction in energy load is the very careful work of the construction team. Nearly every supplier of building products for the exterior envelope retooled the manufacturing of their components to help achieve the project goals. The superbly sealed, triple-glazed windows have been fitted with great care, and very high-quality detailing and construction of the enclosure has been achieved throughout, resulting in a completely draught-free envelope for maximum comfort in the cold winter months.

The Hudson House exceeded its project goals, primarily by virtue of the execution of its construction. The project was modelled to achieve an air test result of $0.6h^{-1}$ @50Pa, but the construction details proved to be more "'user friendly'" for the builder than anticipated so a truly excellent $0.15h^{-1}$ @50Pa was achieved. The result was that in its first winter of operation, no supplementary heating at all was required by the occupants.

It's a great credit to the team that the results of this research project have been incorporated into a training programme that teaches architects, engineers, building scientists, and builders, the methods of Passive House design and construction.

Location	Claverack, New York, US
Date	2011
Client	Private
Team	Architect: BarlisWedlick Architects, formerly Dennis Wedlick Architects Services engineer: The Levy Partnership Structural engineer: Engineering Ventures Cost Consultant: Dennis Wedlick Passive House consultant: Dennis Wedlick Contractor: Bill Stratton Building Company
Energy	12.1kWh/m²/yr specific space-heating demand (predicted)
Air test	$0.15h^{-1}$ (50Pa pressure difference)

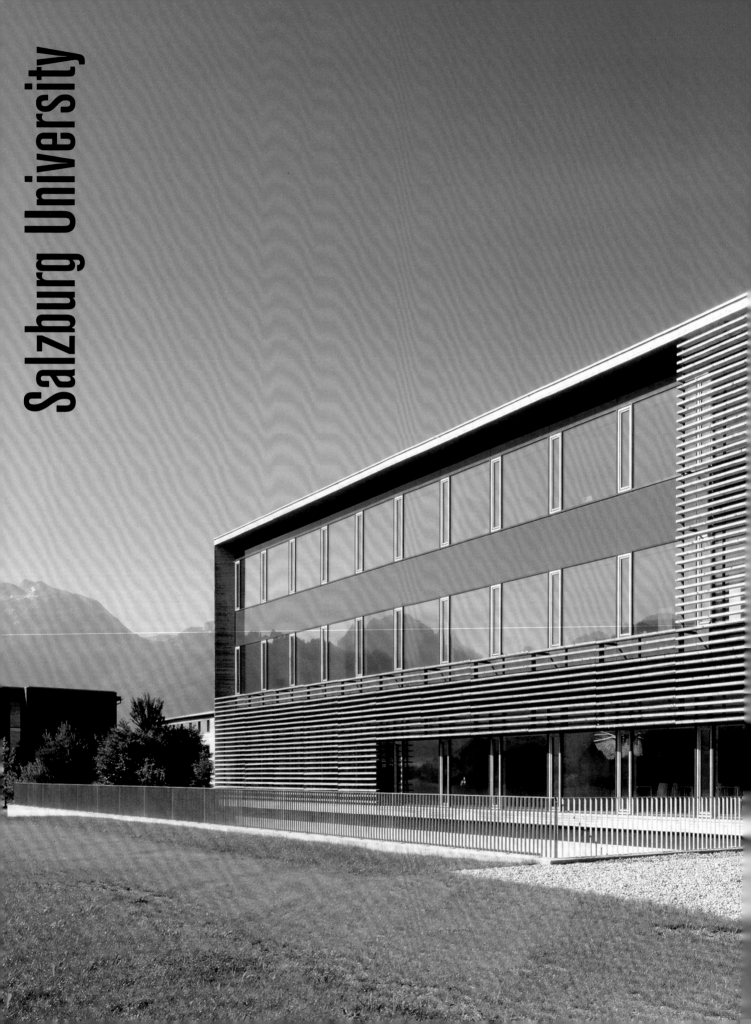

Salzburg University

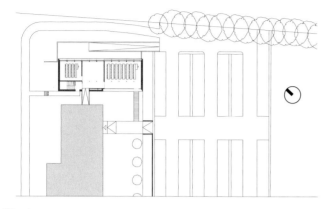

Site plan

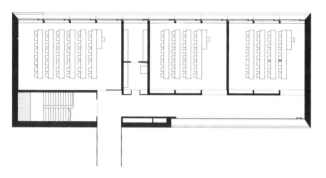

Second-floor plan

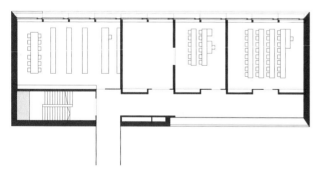

First-floor plan

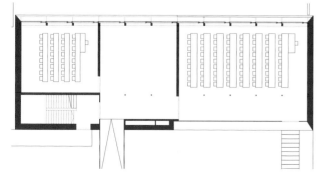

Ground-floor plan

Background

The extension to the Kuchl Campus of the Salzburg University of Applied Sciences is a state-of-the-art building both in terms of timber engineering construction and in the fact that it is Austria's first institute of higher education building to implement Passive House technology.

I first saw the beautiful work of Dietrich | Untertrifaller when I visited their secondary school at Klaus during the International Passive House Conference held at Bregenz in 2007. This showed me how Passive House architecture can be executed to a high level of refinement. Such work is very much of its time and place. Vorarlberg politicians, professionals and public have spent the last few decades on a sustainability and self-sufficiency drive, which has resulted in a rapid growth of local skilled tradespeople and manufacturers producing the necessary goods for a sustainable local economy. A steady demand for these commodities has enabled investment in product research and development, so that some of the best and most sustainable goods in Europe are now produced in the region. As exports have increased so have the skills of the workforce, to the point at which Passive House design and exceptionally beautiful aesthetics are now the new vernacular of the country.

Brief

The extension to the Kuchl campus was completed as a modern timber construction in September 2009. The vision was that the students would be able to engage in their studies while absorbing the institute's ideals of "timber, design and sustainability". The university's own building was to serve as a "best practice example" in Kuchl – and what better way to spread this vision into the community than to give 400 students the positive benefit and experience of using this building every day for their studies?

The design

The campus, surrounded by farmland, is located approximately one kilometre north-east of Kuchl's centre. The campus area borders the forestry academy to the north and a student dormitory to the south. The adjacent, existing building was completed in 1995. Its central access corridor connects to the new building via a glazed service bridge.

A large art room on the ground floor, accommodating 200 people, is illuminated from both sides. On the upper floors, a wide corridor finished with floor-to-ceiling glass behind south-west-facing timber louvres provides access to seminar rooms and the library. The main glazed elevation of the building faces north-east. At night, the floors of this elevation seem to float unsupported above the site.

The building is made of timber on the inside and outside. The floors are made from huge, prefabricated, timber-box elements, with laminated timber beams and panels acting together and interlocking like three-dimensional

jigsaw pieces. Six slender, steel columns complement the timber frame, which is connected together by metal flitch plates and brackets. Suspended ceilings and framed walls are all clad with precisely jointed, oiled birch plywood. The concrete escape staircase acts as a stabilising core. Cross-laminated timber is used sparingly to demonstrate a wise use of precious resources; only the two full-height end walls are made from the material, in order to provide the necessary sheer stiffness to the structure.

Evaluation

Building with prefabricated timber elements, when done with such refinement, is very convincing. The Salzburg University of Applied Sciences has successfully implemented a functional and beautiful multistorey timber construction according to the Passive House standard, which uses less than 15kWh/m² of heating and cooling energy per year.

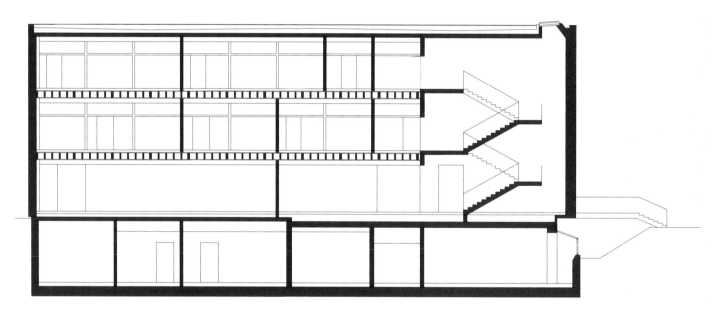

Section

Location	Markt, Kuchl, Austria
Date	2009
Client	Fachhochschule Salzburg (Salzburg University of Applied Sciences)
Team	Architect: Dietrich | Untertrifaller Services engineer: Burggraf Structural engineer (timber): Pock Structural engineer (concrete): Gaderer Passive House consultant: Graml Contractor: Weco FH Holztechnikum
Energy	10.0kWh/m²/yr specific space-heating demand
Air test	0.49h⁻¹ (50Pa pressure difference)

Villa Langenkamp

Background

This uncomplicated and contemporary design is built from prefabricated timber elements. The house has a compact geometry and clean, horizontal lines that sit beautifully in the wooded landscape of tall, majestic pines and long horizons. The sleek architectural design, the solar panels on the roof and the negligible energy consumption all speak of a functional yet minimal house adapted to the urgent need to design for minimal energy requirements.

Brief

At first, a two-storey design was considered because of the energy benefits of a compact form, and in order to split the spatial layout into social rooms on the ground floor and more private rooms on the first floor. However, the concept adopted in the end is that all the functions are contained and integrated in one unified, regular shape, resulting in a beautiful, economical, simple design.

Ideally, a northern-hemisphere passive house would be oriented towards south to gain optimum benefit from the sun. However, because the best views here are towards the west, and also to follow the layout of the site, the Villa Langenkamp faces west. This required the design to provide compensation by optimising other low-energy features.

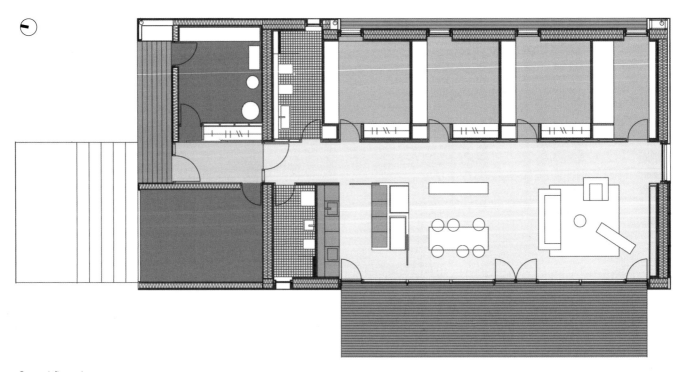

Ground-floor plan

The design

Although the parts of the house on the northern side – with its porch, garage, entrance and plant room – are fully integrated into the overall appearance, they lie outside the Passive House envelope.

Once inside the Passive House envelope, the plan is disposed about a longitudinal axis that subdivides the spaces between living and sleeping. To the west, the house opens up into one large space containing the living room and kitchen, with the enclosed bedroom units to the east. The morning sun enters the bedrooms, and around midday an "axis of light" divides the bedrooms from the living area. During the afternoon and evening, the sunlight strikes the west facade and paints streaks of light on the interior through the blinds of the solar shading.

The house is very well insulated. U-values are 0.05 W/(m²K) for the roof and floor, and 0.09 W/(m²K) for the exterior walls. Retractable exterior blinds provide summer solar shading. Hot water is produced by 8m² of solar collectors on the roof, backed up by a heat pump. Air for the ventilation system is preheated as required and pre-warmed by means of 30m of earth tubes buried at a depth of 1.80m around the building, through which all the inlet air passes before entering the building. A red-coloured, honeycomb-like pattern of card panels behind the south facing wall of glass at the end of the house allows the low winter sun to pass through it to heat the interior, while the pattern provides some shade from the high summer sun

Evaluation

The strict geometry of this lovely house contrasts with its organic surroundings, and yet the simple box shape settles into and harmonises with the landscape. This elegant building shows how to integrate high-performance design with deliberate simplicity of form to achieve economical yet highly refined architecture.

Section

Location	Tigervej, Ebeltoft, Denmark
Date	2008
Client	Private
Team	Architect: Olav Langenkamp Services engineer: Passivhus.dk Structural engineer: Ökologischer Holzbau Sellstedt Passive House consultant: Søren Pedersen Contractor: Ökologischer Holzbau Sellstedt (ÖHB)
Energy	11.0kWh/m²/yr specific space-heating demand (predicted)
Air test	0.6h⁻¹ (50pa pressure difference)

Mayville Community Centre

Background

The Mayville Community Centre is a retrofit of a 19th-century building located in the heart of a deprived social-housing estate in north-east London. Recently renamed the Mildmay Centre, it is the first non-domestic Passive House retrofit in the UK. As such it is an important model for deep retrofits of old, solid-walled buildings, demonstrating how this common building typology – a medium-sized, Victorian masonry building – can be transformed to achieve energy-consumption reductions that greatly improve upon all current and planned UK Building Regulations standards.

Brief

The Mayville Community Partnership (MCP) needed to try to find a solution to its energy costs, which, at £10,000 a year, were unsustainable for a community organisation with an annual turnover of just £70,000. The centre accepted the architect's proposal for a deep Passive House retrofit and a complete reorganisation and refurbishment of the building, including the conversion of a cold and draughty basement. MCP then set about raising 100% of the funding needed for an ambitious new project to transform the building.

The design

Refurbishment focused on providing more usable space through efficient internal replanning, and by excavating outside the south elevation to create new space in the basement without increasing the building footprint.

The building has massive 450mm-thick walls of solid brickwork. Although its embodied energy is high, solid brick is an easily maintained and repaired material, and, already in existence, it made sense to retain the original fabric of the building. The strategy was quite simple: wrap the existing walls and roof structure in external insulation and replace all windows with Passive House certified, triple-glazed windows. External, retractable blinds control overheating in summer.

Winter ventilation is achieved on the basis of "ventilating the occupants", which means that the ventilation runs only during hours of occupancy in order to avoid wasting energy. The main hall and the dining room are both areas of variable occupancy, and in these spaces CO_2 sensors boost the ventilation when required in order to maintain excellent winter air quality. Summer ventilation is achieved by opening tilt-and-turn windows, which can also be used for night-time purge ventilation.

With the building's energy demand dramatically reduced, renewable technologies for electricity and hot water became more significant as a proportion of the total energy consumption. A photovoltaic array with a peak production capability of 18kWp and a solar thermal panel were installed on the main roof for electricity and hot water, whilst the minimal heat demand is achieved via a

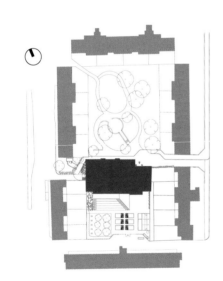

Site plan

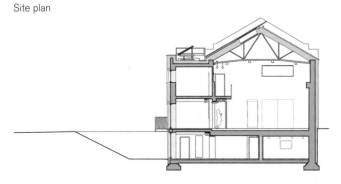

Section

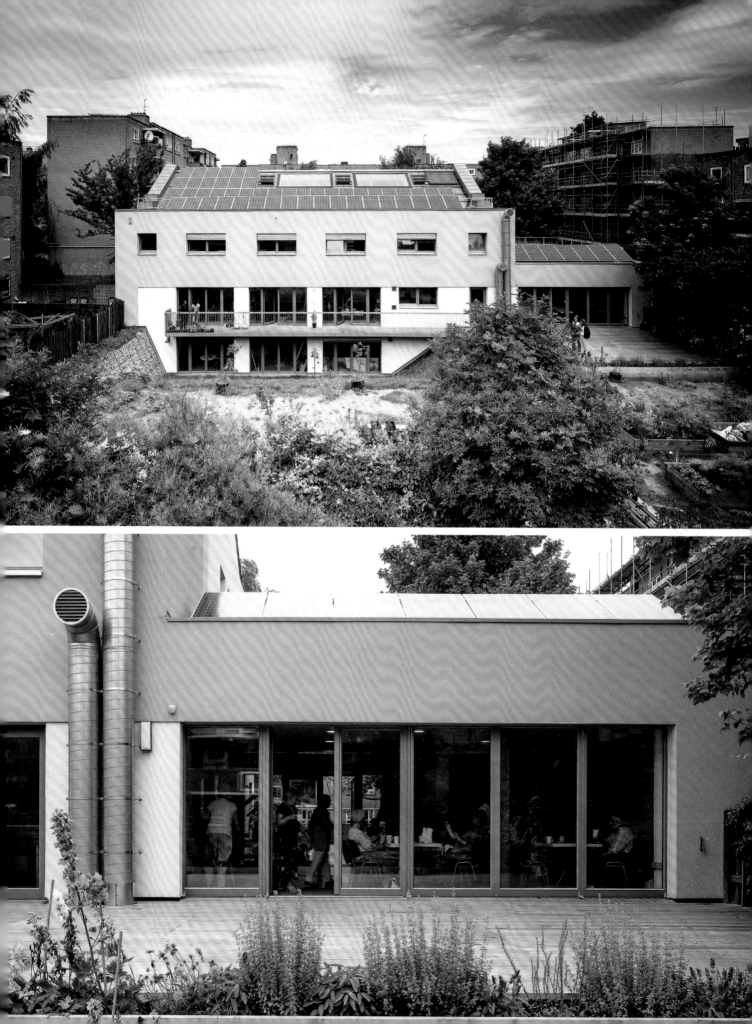

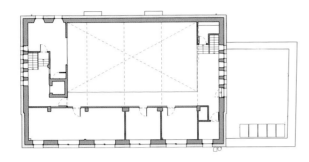

First-floor plan

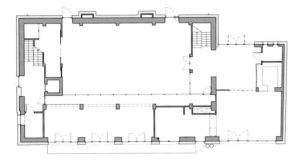

Ground-floor plan

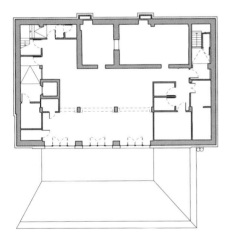

Basement-floor plan

Location	Woodville Road, London, UK
Date	2011
Client	Mildmay Community Partnership
Team	Architect: bere:architects Services engineer: Alan Clarke Structural engineer: Conisbee PHPP calculations: bere:architects Cost consultant: Richard Whidborne Ventilation design: Green Building Store Contractor: Buxtons Windows: Doublegood (Bayer)
Energy	13.0kWh/m²/yr specific space-heating demand (predicted)
Air test	0.43h⁻¹ (50Pa pressure difference)

ground-source heat pump that supplies heat to a low-temperature radiator circuit. Two rainwater harvesting tanks collect 11,000 litres of rainwater for WC flushing and garden irrigation. Native meadow roofs have been installed to provide a wildlife habitat and reduce rainwater run-off. Bird boxes have been installed within the external insulation layer.

Low-energy lighting is switched on and off manually, with override via PIR presence sensors. Micro bore hot-water pipes minimise standing pipe losses. To keep the controls as simple as possible, the design team avoided a complex building management system (BMS). The building's controls are almost as simple as those of a domestic house.

Evaluation

The Mayville Community Centre has been given a grant for two years' of building performance evaluation undertaken with the BSRIA (Building Services Research and Information Association) and funded by the UK's Technology Strategy Board. Operational results during its first winter showed 95% overall energy savings compared with previous overall performance. Over its entire first year of monitoring, 80% overall energy savings have been achieved. Due to higher occupancy than expected, the building has lower heating demand than predicted and at the same time comfort conditions have been greatly improved. Elderly residents say that in winter they feel warm enough, for the first time, to be able to remove their coats during their social gatherings. This was achieved for an additional 8% costs over a standard refurbishment, or just 3% if a basic Passive House without renewable technologies had been required.

Conclusions

A beautiful solution

This book has attempted to show why Passive House is the best form of building for people's health, comfort and general wellbeing, for every age group, for fantastically low energy use, for very low whole-life costs, for the environment as a whole and for the future of the planet.

If I had one objective when I started writing this book, it was to show that beautiful Passive House buildings can be achieved in all climates around the globe, bringing great comfort and health benefits to people while at the same time looking after the precious ecosystems of this wonderful planet: rich ecosystems, consisting of thousands of species living in symbiosis, that have taken hundreds of millions of years to develop and that are right now being destroyed by our own species in a matter of just a few generations. We are in the midst of the biggest process of mass extinction that has ever occurred on this planet. However, I still believe that the individual has huge power to effect change; to demonstrate to the wider community that we can live in harmony with the world, which is our cradle; that we need not destroy Mother Nature; that sustainable living is affordable (indeed, we cannot afford any other option); and that we can derive huge pleasure in enjoying a solution in our homes, and in our non-domestic buildings too, that works for us now and for future generations.

I agree with Bill Bordass that we are in the "Last Chance Saloon". Carbon emissions continue to rise globally while scientists tell us they must be reduced dramatically to minimise the risk of catastrophic climate change. But once again, new sources of harmful, polluting energy are emerging. Fossil-fuel extraction and supply is as profitable as it is irresponsible and dangerous for the future of life on this planet. There is a real danger that as one country delivers new sources of fossil fuel to its citizens, people will succumb to one of the most primitive instincts – that of competition. However, with each dash for fossil fuel we are all brought ever closer to economic and environmental catastrophe. If we are to survive as a species, our civilisations must become focused on reducing energy demand by competing to urgently deliver efficiency and a zero-carbon electricity grid, which will eventually produce, free, clean energy sufficient to supply new low-energy lifestyles. As individuals, we can demonstrate in our own lives that it's possible to reduce our carbon footprint to sustainable levels and that we can expect very comfortable and healthy buildings without them "costing the earth".

As this book has shown, the economics of Passive House are clear. While shifting priorities is a simple lifestyle choice for many, for others the help of responsible, intelligent and forward-looking governments is needed in order to make it easy for individuals and organisations to make steps now, for the benefits of both themselves and of society at large, now and in the future.

So what is most important now is to consider the implications of in-use performance data from Passive House buildings. The evidence so far is that to provide comfort, to save energy, to reduce bills, to protect people from fuel poverty, to reduce excess winter deaths, to save money in the long run and, arguably most importantly, to reduce CO_2 emissions, it is difficult to escape the conclusion that deep, energy-saving Passive House retrofits and new-builds must become the norm. A deep, energy-saving retrofit programme will create jobs now at the same time as saving money on fuel imports, both now and long into the future. Vast amounts of money can also be saved by reducing the need for new power stations and for long-term storage of nuclear waste, and by reducing the serious impact upon the National Health Service of the UK's dreadful, damp and draughty buildings.

We now know the excellent results that are consistently and affordably achieved in actual use by Passive House buildings across the UK. Great results and great occupant feedback keep rolling in to us and to others who are building and monitoring Passive House buildings. The international and UK Passive House community has already done the groundwork in this respect. It's now over to those with the power to roll out change across the country, and in conclusion I will repeat the question that visitors to Passive House buildings seem to ask more than any other: **Why aren't all buildings built like this?**

Further Information

The Passivhaus Institut

The Passivhaus Institut (PHI) of Darmstadt, Germany, is an independent research institute. It is led by its founder, Dr Wolfgang Feist, with a continuously growing interdisciplinary team, currently of more than 40 employees. The institute is constantly developing and improving upon algorithms and software tools for dynamic building simulations, the determination of energy balances by means of software such as the Passive House Planning Package (PHPP), and the planning of Passive House buildings. I would like to thank the Passivhaus Insitut for their assistance in publishing this book and for kindly allowing us to reproduce some of their diagrams and graphs.

The International Passive House Association

The International Passive House Association (IPHA) has been set up by the Passivhaus Institut to provide technical support to people around the world. The IPHA is helping to set up local training and membership groups. The Irish Passive House Academy holds training courses for consultants and contractors in Ireland and the US; the Building Research Establishment (BRE) and AECB/Warm Consulting both offer training courses in the UK, as well as certification.

The Passive House Planning Package (PHPP)

PHPP software is the product of many thousands of hours of development work by scientists at the Passivhaus Institut in Germany and at universities, particularly in Germany and Austria. PHPP is based upon dynamic building-simulation models, which the PHI is constantly developing and improving upon. PHPP is open-source software at its very best, and researchers and students from around the world are now working on integrating PHPP into commercially available Building Information Management (BIM) digital drawing packages such as Archicad, Revit and SketchUp. One of the first universities to publish their research was Parsons the New School for Design, New York, in collaboration with the Stevens Institute of Technology and Habitat for Humanity of Washington DC. Their work focused on automatically translating information from a 3D Rhino model into PHPP. Then at the International Passive House Conference in 2012, we heard about a promising collaboration in BIM between the Danish Passive House Centre (the certification organisation for Denmark) and Bjerg Arkitecktur, who are developing links between Revit and PHPP – as are others in the US and Europe. Currently the PHI is developing a link between PHPP and Google SketchUp.

Passivhaus-Bauteilkatalog

Details for Passive Houses – An invaluable catalogue of ecologically rated construction details, published by IBO, the Austrian Institute for Healthy and Ecological Building.

Passipedia

The Passive House knowledge database.
www.passipedia.org

Regional Passive House Associations

IG Passivhaus Deutschland, Germany

Passivhaus Trust, United Kingdom

Passive House Association of Ireland (PHAI)

Passzívházépítok Országos Szövetsége (PAOSZ), Hungary

IG Passivhus Sverige, Sweden

NY Passive House (NYPH), USA

Passive House Institute New Zealand (PHINZ)

Inštitút pre energeticky pasívne domy (iEPD) Slovakia

Zero Energy and PassivHaus Institute for Research (ZEPHIR), Italy

Dansk Passivhus Forum (DPHF), Denmark

Passive House Association of Estonia

Passive House California (PHCa), United States

Associação Passivhaus Portugal (PHPT)

Plataforma PEP Spain

Passivhaus Austria

Picture Credits

Achim Grosee/Ackerman+Raff GmbH & Co. KG
pp. 44-45, 47, 49

Ackerman+Raff GmbH & Co. KG
pp. 46, 48

Architekten Hermann Kaufmann ZT GmbH
pp. 58, 60, 61

ArchitekturWerkstatt Vallentin
pp. 88, 90

Architype
pp. 43, 78, 80

BarlisWedlick Architects LLC
pp. 100, 102

be baumschlager eberle
pp. 96, 98

bere:architects
pp. 7, 10, 11, 17, 18, 19, 22, 24-25, 27 (chart - middle, photo - right), 29 (charts), 31, 35 (photos), 37, 38, 39, 74, 76, 114, 116, 117

Bill Bordass
p. 27 (chart, top)

Bruno Klomfar Photography
pp. 56-57, 59, 62, 63, 104-105, 107, 109

Calderon-Folch-Sarsanedas Arquitectes SLP/Pol Viladoms
p. 23 (left)

Christine Blaser, Bildaufbau-Fotografie
pp. 50-51, 53, 55

Cukrowicz Nachbaur Architekten
pp. 84, 86

Dan Hanes/bere:architects
pp. 29 (photo)

Dietrich | Untertrifaller Architekten ZT GmbH
pp. 106, 108

D'Inka Scheible Hoffmann Architekten BDA
pp. 70, 71

Edward Hueber/Archphoto
pp. 97, 99

Eight Associates for Paul Davis and Partners
p. 35 (chart)

Elia Sterling (*eliasterling206@gmail.com*)
p. 36

Elliott Kaufman Photography
pp. 101, 103 (bottom 2 images)

Erica Overmeer/ Future Documentation
pp. 93, 95

Gaia Architects
p. 43

Gavin Phillips/Hawkes Architecture Ltd
p. 42

Halle 58 Architekten
pp. 52, 54

Hanspeter Schiess Fotografie
pp. 82–83, 85, 87

Institut Wohnen und Umwelt, Darmstadt, Germany
p. 15 (photo, left)

Jacob Kanzleiter
pp. 89, 91

*Jefferson Smith/*bere:architects
pp. 77 (2 on right)

Käferstein & Meister Architekten
pp. 92, 94

Key Architects
pp. 64, 65, 66, 67

Langenkamp.dk Architects
pp. 4–5, 110, 111, 112, 113

Leigh Simpson Photographer
pp. 79, 81

Passivhaus Institut
pp.14, 15 (photo, right), 20
Based on graphics by the Passivhaus Institut, pp.15 (charts) 16, 25

PAUL Wärmerückgewinnung GmbH
p. 21

Peter Aaron/OTTO
p. 103 (top)

Roland Halbe Fotografie
pp. 68-69, 71, 73

Seymour-Smith Architects
p. 42

Skellefteå Power
p. 13

Stahl-Weiss
p. 40

Sturgis Carbon Profiling
pp. 32, 33

Tim Crocker/bere:architects
pp. 75, 77 (3 on left), 115, 117

Timothy/BMeiA
p. 23 (right)

Thomas Stoney Bryans
p. 30